Gridlock

in

Government

Gridlock in Government:
How to Break the Stagnation of America

Roger E. Meiners
and
Roger LeRoy Miller

Published by the Free Congress Foundation, Washington,
D.C., in cooperation with the State Policy Network, 1518
Washington Street, Columbia, SC 29201; 803-779-5022.

The opinions in this book are solely those of the authors.
This book is an educational resource; it is not intended to
influence legislation before Congress or any state
legislature.

ISBN 0–942522–20–6

PREFACE

The American people determine the fate of the nation. The public has become increasingly disgusted with the government and is distressed about the lack of economic progress. The appeal of Ross Perot reflected that unhappiness—huge numbers of people are telling Republicans and Democrats that they are fed up with the politics of those parties. The disgust with politics is real but unfortunate. Politics is serious business because it determines our future.

Thirty years ago, 25% of the voters said that government is pretty much run by special interests looking out for themselves; in 1992, 80% of the voters say that special interests, not the will of the people, determine policies. Voter outrage leads to grass roots movements. The push for term limits is such a movement. Term limits comes from the people. It is resisted by many politicians and their special interest friends; it is ignored by the media elite and most academics. But the people are *right*; we need term limits. This book explains why.

We would like to thank the Cain Foundation, McCamish Foundation, Roe Foundation, Scaife Foundation, and the State Policy Network for their support of this project. Roger Meiners would like to thank the Political Economy Research Center of Bozeman, Montana, for hosting his sabbatical stay in 1992 so that he could work on this book. Many people provided us assistance in gathering information helpful in the preparation of this book.

Finally we want to thank and salute the many citizens who have taken the lead in getting something done about term limits in their states. This is true citizen participation in the democratic process; there is no reward for these people except the satisfaction they have of knowing that they have done their part to make their country a better place.

TABLE OF CONTENTS

Chapter 1   Where Is America Headed?   1

Chapter 2   Lifetime Politicians Who   6
             Stand Only for Themselves

Chapter 3   Government Growing Like Topsy   14

Chapter 4   Is the American Dream Over?   24

Chapter 5   Where Does It All Go?   34

Chapter 6   The Deficit and the Debt   41

Chapter 7   The Public Debt Albatross   53

Chapter 8   The Same Old Song   64

Chapter 9   Prime the Pump?   74

Chapter 10   Who Pays What?   86

Chapter 11   Preying on the Poor   93

Chapter 12   Resegregating America   102

Chapter 13   Throw the Rascals Out   111

Chapter 14   Why Term Limits?   120

Chapter 15   Term Limits Are Happening!   133

             Data Sources   143

             About the Authors   149

Chapter 1

Where Is America Headed?

As the year 2000 nears, we will see articles and books with such titles as, "The Next Millennium: What Does It Mean?", and other important sounding "predictions" about how the world will be different. But January 1, 2000, is just another day. Other than getting used to writing a strange number on checks, there is no reason to think that the world will be different just because it is the first day of a new millennium. Nevertheless, events such as this one do give pause for thought. Where have we been and where are we going?

America has the most amazing history of any nation in the modern world. For most people in the world, America has been, as President Reagan said, a shining city on the hill. Regardless of how others see America, most of us who *are* Americans do not think of ourselves as living in a shining city on a hill. We lead our lives and get along as best we can. Things could be better or worse for all of us.

In 1980, Ronald Reagan asked the American voters if they were better off than they were four years before, when Jimmy Carter became president. They said no, and they were right. The sad thing is that if you ask if average

Americans are better off today than they were 20 years ago, the answer is also no. Despite our great history, recent history has not been kind to America. **For over 20 years now we have been in** *gridlock*—**our political system is wedded to a host of government policies that are causing our economy to spin its wheels.**

No Joy in Mudville

In the past few years the Soviet empire has collapsed. This was an extraordinary event that was not predicted to happen. Hundreds of millions of people have been made free to chart their future and the world is mostly free of the threat of nuclear war. But this startling event seems mostly to have been forgotten. Maybe instant television, which can show us smart bombs going through doors in buildings in Iraq, has made us immune to the importance of truly historic events. Things that startle us one minute are old news the next day. While the fall of communism in eastern Europe and the old USSR may be old news, this is nonetheless a great time in history.

The world now has a greater chance for more free economies to allow more people to enjoy decent standards of living in democratic countries than ever before. Democracy and the wealth from open economies is no longer only available to the people of a few nations in Europe, North America, and the Pacific Rim—it has the chance to happen worldwide. This means that Americans no longer have to bear the high cost of defending the free world. We will have more resources to spend on things besides military hardware; we will have more trading partners in a wealthier world. **Peace and freedom exist for more people than ever before in history.**

While Americans enjoyed the fall of the Berlin wall and wish the peoples of the former "evil empire" well, there is not the kind of joy we would have expected to result from such wondrous events. **America is not a happy nation; the people sense there is something wrong with our government and its policies that demands fundamental change. The people are right.**

No Future in the Stars

Some people think the stars can tell them about the future. Other people think they can foresee the future. We do not know anyone who has ever been good at consistently predicting the future—and we know we can't. So this book is not the story of what is going to happen in the year 2000. We are not predicting a long–run boom or a bust economy because we do not think either is likely. But neither are we very optimistic about what the future holds.

Our political system is gridlocked. The net result is big government tied to special interests and entitlement programs that pay something to almost everyone. Why we have gotten into this situation is not clear. American history has been one of long–run growth that has raised living standards for all citizens. That is not happening in this generation and it looks worse for the next. **Unless there are basic changes in our political institutions that will allow our economy to grow again, America will wallow in its own muddle and jealously watch many nations pass us in their standard of living.**

Most nations end up in a mess that outsiders can see quite clearly, but those in the middle of a mess cannot. Telling foreigners how to sort things out and get on the right track is not easy because nations are complicated. We have a hard enough time trying to make our own families work well; trying to make a nation run like a Swiss (or Japanese) watch is a feat no one person or group of persons can do, let alone comprehend.

No, Virginia, There Is No Santa Claus

The story we tell in the rest of this book outlines the extent of American political gridlock that has stopped this nation's previous gradual march of progress. This is not a happy story to tell but is based on our collective 50 years of studying and writing about political economy.

This book will not explain how to make America run smoothly. As much as we would like to think that there is a simple answer or that there is one person who can make things right, we are old enough to know that there is no Santa and he certainly does not live in Washington, D.C. **As Americans, we will either sort out the mess we are in by the rough justice of democratic politics, or we will live in a slowly deteriorating nation.**

Breaking the Gridlock

To rejuvenate the economy and provide more opportunities for all, we have to break the gridlock that has made our government resistant to reform. The special interests that dominate what emerges from Congress will oppose change. Because special interests are organized and well–funded, and know what they are about, we must attack the root of the problem—the perverse incentives that cause good people in politics to go bad.

As we will discuss in this book, politicians understand the gridlock that is choking our economy and preventing imaginative reform in government. These are not issues that can be solved by intellectual debate. Members of Congress are intelligent people who are better informed about problems and possible solutions than almost anyone else. **We cannot ask politicians to do things that are not in their own interest—which is reelection for life.**

To have a chance at substantive reforms emerging from

Congress and state legislatures, the hold of special interests must be weakened. Our representatives must be given incentives to address problems as they best think they can be solved. We will show that term limits is a powerful constitutional change that will give America a chance to be the shining city on the hill in the next millennium.

Chapter 2

Lifetime Politicians
Who Stand
Only for Themselves

Before the election in 1990, only 23% of voters surveyed said they approved of the job Congress is doing. Yet 96% of all incumbents returned to Congress after the election. Respect for Congress is even lower in 1992. Disgust with politics as usual cuts across Republicans, Democrats, and independents. Voters of all backgrounds are fed up. Can things change or are voters acting childishly?

The check–kiting scandal in the House of Representatives, the ability to retire with fat pensions, and the right to keep campaign funds that have been collected will result in more incumbents than usual leaving Congress in 1992. Over 100 of the 435 members of the House will have retired voluntarily or been sent into retirement by the voters.

Political commentators claim this is evidence that term limits are not needed. The voters are disgusted and so there will be high turnover in Congress. These commentators know the news, but they do not understand how the political system works. **The problem we face is not the quality of people who are elected; the problem is the incentives they face after election.**

To focus on the people instead of the incentives that exist in our political system misses the point. Most people who enter politics do so with decent, even admirable, motives. But once they have fulfilled the hard task of capturing a seat in Congress, their attention turns to how to keep their seats. If senators and representatives want to keep their jobs, as most do, they must single–mindedly focus on the process of getting reelected.

The term–limit movement arose because voters understand this perverse incentive structure faced by their representatives. Elected officials who try to act in the best interests of the nation (as they see those interests) rather than in the best interests of the people who get them elected and reelected, are likely to be *ex*–officials. **Political competition means elected officials must sacrifice principle in favor of constituent service and serving special interests.**

The Irrelevance of Ideology

Successful politicians rarely stand by ideological principles when political gain is at stake. Ideology itself is important. It can be helpful to know if a politician is a liberal, a conservative, a socialist, a libertarian, or follows another philosophy. Indeed, such labels *used* to be meaningful. One could generally guess where a Franklin Roosevelt or a Ronald Reagan stood. In contrast, George Bush, like most politicians, has no ideological roots.

Today, with few exceptions, there is no liberal–versus–conservative debate of a serious nature. Those terms are used for window dressing to mask the details of special–interest legislation. Members of Congress make most decisions based on what they perceive will serve the interests of constituents in their districts.

Representative Newt Gingrich of Georgia and Senator

Jesse Helms of North Carolina are portrayed by the press as free–market conservatives. No doubt they are, in their heart–of–hearts. But they vote for special interest programs such as textile protection, tobacco allotments, and sugar subsidies in order to be re–elected. These votes contradict their free–market rhetoric. **Unless there is a change in incentives, politicians must serve special interests to survive politically.**

Strom Thurmond ran for President in 1948 as a third party candidate to oppose efforts to end legal racial segregation. In the Senate he fought civil rights legislation for years. But once blacks became voters in large numbers in South Carolina, Thurmond knew he had to work for legislation that would benefit black voters in South Carolina. He was so successful that he won a higher percentage of black voters when he was reelected in 1984 than any Republican senator in the nation.

Remember the "Reagan Revolution" that was supposed to have arrived in the 1980 election? It would bring the federal government "under control." Agencies would be abolished, regulations would be rolled back, and spending would be cut. We have no doubt that Ronald Reagan wanted to accomplish those things. But even if the president is ideological—conservative in Reagan's case—it is Congress, responding to special interests, that is supreme.

So, even when the Senate was controlled by Republicans, and Congress had been shocked by the number of incumbents defeated in 1980, major changes proposed by Reagan were rejected by Congress. **Because politicians want to be reelected over and over, decisions are determined by special–interest groups that provide the resources needed for reelection; serious debates about issues matter little.**

Intractable Incumbents

In some years the reelection rate for members of Congress has run as high as 98 percent, even though the polls consistently show that the public is fed up with Congress. Such consistent reelection is rational. Most senators and representatives are doing a good job for their states and districts, given the way Congress works. They got elected and get reelected by serving constituents and special interests. There is nothing really wrong with the individuals that voters send to Washington. It is the system that needs reform.

What would happen if voters in one state threw out their representatives every election? They would have no seniority or committee assignments in Congress that help get special benefits for their districts. These "goodies" come with long tenure in Congress. The renegade state would get fewer benefits shipped to it from Congress. Voters are sensible when they return representatives to Washington over and over.

To *get* along you have to *go* along. When you want goodies, you vote for other people's goodies. There is no reward for *not* voting for goodies. The representatives from other states surely will be happy to grab all they can for their home folks. People who go to Congress with fine ideals learn that the easiest way, and maybe the only way, to stay in their seats is to cater to special interests.

The record on this point is clear. Look at the voting records of members of Congress. On average, the longer people are in Congress, the more spending they vote for. The National Taxpayers Union publishes an annual score of "fiscal conservatism" based on votes on taxes and spending. For the 12 years from 1978 to 1989, members of the House of Representatives for more than 12 years (6 terms) voted in favor of taxes and spending 18.4% more often than did the representatives there for less than 12 years. **Regardless of party, the longer people are in Congress—or a state legislature—the more they are likely to become big spenders of taxpayers' money.**

Another voting index, produced by the Competitive Enterprise Institute, looks at votes for pork barrel spending—federal dollars going for special interest causes rather than the general public. The members of the House of Representatives who voted the most *against* pork had an average tenure of 8 years. In contrast, members of the House who voted *for* the most pork spending had an average tenure of 17 years. These numbers are true for Democrats and Republicans. **Regardless of party, the longer one is in Congress the better pork barrel spending is likely to look.**

They *All* Do It

Remember the famous "Read my lips, no new taxes" promise of George Bush in 1988 that he broke in 1990? That tax hike was passed by a narrow vote in Congress. People who had been in the House more than 12 years favored the tax hike by 86–54; people who had been in the Senate more than 12 years favored it by 28–13. People in the House less than 12 years opposed the tax hike 146–142; senators in office for less than 12 years voted against the hike by a vote of 32–26. **Regardless of party, the longer one is in Congress, the more taxes look desirable.**

The incentive to become a big spender–big taxer has little to do with party or ideology. It has to do with a willingness to give every special interest group what it wants in order to maximize the longevity of members of Congress.

Gifts are handed out to a host of business and labor union interests. In return come campaign contributions and votes. Anyone who thinks that liberal Democrats are tough on special interests has been listening to what they say, *not watching what they do.*

Some of the most left–wing members of Congress, such as Barney Frank of Massachusetts, who scored 100% in the voting index published by the liberal Americans for Democratic Action (ADA) in 1986, joined nine other 100% liberals in four key votes for subsidies for business that year. They voted for cut–rate loans to needy companies such as Hyatt, Holiday Inn, and Hilton; a trust fund for companies hurt by international competition; subsidized loans for ordinary businesses; and funds for development of private golf courses and tourist attractions.

These votes may explain why business does not rush to fund the opponents of supposedly "left–wing" Congressmen such as Barney Frank. In 1990, Mr. Frank had 22 times more campaign contributions than his more conservative opponent. Congressman Henry Waxman of California, another 100% ADA–rated liberal, does not worry about corporate contributions rushing to help his competitor. Mr. Waxman raked in over $300,000 in political action committee (PAC) contributions in 1990; his opponent could not scrape together $2,000.

Another member of Congress with a reputation as a "watchdog" is John Dingell of Michigan. In 1990, he had over $840,000 to spend on his way to his 36th year in the House. Three–quarters of this money came from PACs; less than 5% of his support came from individual contributions of $200 or less. The Republican he slaughtered had less than 1/2% of that amount to spend.

Special interests do not fight those who supposedly make their lives hard. In 1990, House incumbents were given over $87 million in contributions by PACs, the main source of special interest money. PACs gave House challengers one–tenth of that amount. There is no punishment for being a big–spending liberal. In 1990, the 15 top PAC recipients in the House were rated an average of 69% liberal by the ADA. On average, they had been in the House for 17 years. **It pays to spend other people's money in Congress; you get to come back and do it again and again.**

Political Gridlock

Politics has become gridlocked. What are portrayed as big differences between "conservatives" and "liberals" look like fights over nickels to foreigners who look at the American scene. The budget battles that make the difference between being a big spender and a tight–fisted conservative are usually votes over a trivial share of the budget. **Votes in Congress are not to decide if major programs are scrapped or kept; most choices are between big budget increases and even bigger budget increases.**

When Congress looks at government programs, the focus is on how much to spend, not whether the program even makes sense. A study by political scientist James Payne looked at Congressional program hearings in the House and Senate from 1983 to 1987, years in which the Democrats controlled the House and the Republicans controlled the Senate. Witnesses who testify before Congressional committees are all invited by the committee. **Over 95% of all witnesses testified in favor of the program under consideration—fewer than 1% were opposed to the programs or to more spending. The system is rigged in one direction.**

Many senators and representatives know that our government is gridlocked. They know there are better solutions to many problems we face. But to advocate real change is risky. It means telling established special interests that there will be fewer goodies for them.

Some politicians manage to sound as if they advocate real change, but that is usually skilled rhetoric. They pretend to be the outsider with fresh views, when the reality is more of the same. Senators and representatives know what the game is about better than anyone. They have won the game; they have no reason to change the game they know how to win. **Unless we change the incentives of elected officials so they have less reason to cater to special interests in order to stay in Congress for a life-long career, the gridlock will not be broken.**

Chapter 3

Government Growing Like Topsy

At the current growth rate, around the year 2000 half our National Income will be spent by our governments. **Unless there are major changes in the structure of our government programs, our children have a bleak economic future.**

Let's look at the size and growth of government—how much money our governments spend today and how that came about. In the next chapters we will look at where the government spends money, our tax burdens, the deficit and the national debt, and what it all means to the future of our economy.

The federal government will spend $1.5 trillion in 1992. That money comes out of our National Income of $4.8 trillion. **The federal government will spend 31 cents of every dollar of income in the economy.**

While we usually talk about spending as a share of Gross Domestic Product (GDP), a more accurate measure of government spending is as a share of National Income. National Income is composed of all wages (74%); proprietors' and farmers' income (8%), interest earnings (11%), and corporate profits (7%). It differs from GDP because it leaves out consumption of fixed capital and other things that do not count in current income. National Income is what we earn today to have available to spend (or save) today.

Working for the Man

Let's look at what portion of National Income goes to support government spending. For many years the race with the Russians for military superiority meant that as much as one dollar in ten was used to support the military. Now, thankfully, that number is falling. It is down to about one dollar in twenty. But that does not mean that income earners get to keep a larger share of their earnings. Non–military spending keeps going up and up—now taking almost one in every two dollars of earnings. The table shows how much of our National Income has been devoted to all government spending and then subtracts the part devoted to military spending.

NATIONAL INCOME SPENT BY GOVERNMENT (%)

	1960	1970	1980	1990	1995	Change
All Government	31.8	37.3	39.2	41.2	44.2	+39%
Defense	11.3	9.8	6.1	6.7	4.9	−57%
Non–Defense	20.5	27.5	33.1	34.5	39.3	+92%
Education	4.1	6.1	5.5	5.6	6.0	+46%
Soc Sec & Medicare	2.7	4.7	7.5	8.7	10.5	+289%
Public Assistance	1.0	2.6	4.2	3.9	5.0	+400%

For years it was claimed—and some politicians keep saying it today—that if we could reduce military spending there would be plenty of money for other government

programs. Well, military spending now takes a smaller
fraction of our income than it has for over 50 years.
Non–military government spending is now five times as
much as military spending. **Talk about a trade–off between guns and butter is pointless; regardless of how
many guns we buy, Congress keeps spreading more and
more butter.**

As the table shows, the share of National Income going
to military spending is down; the share that goes to non–
defense spending is almost double what it was a generation
ago. Let us look at some of the major parts of non–defense
spending.

We all know the sad story of public education—more
money gets poured in for worse results. While education
spending has risen substantially, its growth pales compared
to the growth in welfare spending and Social Security
benefits. The share of National Income needed to keep the
Social Security system afloat has gone up almost four–fold
over the 35 years viewed here. The. share of National
Income devoted to public assistance (welfare) has gone up
five–fold. **The only boom area of our economy is the
growth of the share of income taken from working
people and given to others in transfer payments—Social
Security and welfare are the largest categories.**

Spending Myths

A gimmick of recent years, that is now treated as a
matter of fact, is to call most of the federal budget "mandatory expenditures" or "entitlements" and to call a smaller
part "discretionary expenditures." This gives the impression
that the president and Congress have little control over the
majority of expenditures.

President Bush proposed a budget for fiscal year 1993
(which begins in 1992) of $1,517 billion dollars. Proposed

budgets are always less than what gets spent, since Congress busts the budget. Look at how the budget was presented. Over half of the budget is called "mandatory expenditures":

PROPOSED 1993 BUDGET ($ billion)

Mandatory expenditures	$766	(51%)
Interest on federal debt	$214	(14%)
Discretionary expenditures	$537	(35%)
TOTAL EXPENDITURES	**$1,517**	**(100%)**

Interest payments on the federal debt really are non–discretionary; the federal government has borrowed trillions of dollars from citizens and foreigners and must pay the interest on that debt or there would be a financial panic. But what about the half of the budget called "mandatory expenditures"? Does the Constitution demand that these expenditures be made? No. **Congress voted for mandatory expenditures and can vote to cut them, just as it can vote to cut discretionary expenditures.**

According to the Omnibus Budget Reconciliation Act of 1990, expenditures in the 1991 budget called "Entitlements and Mandatories" include Social Security, Medicare, Medicaid, food stamps, Aid to Families with Dependent Children (welfare), agriculture subsidies such as the Dairy Indemnity Program, student loans, federal employees' retirement, grants to the states for social services, and, of course, congressional pay.

These expenditures are called entitlements to give the impression that there is a right to payments under these programs. That is not the case; these programs and their spending rules were determined by Congress and can be changed any time Congress has the will to do so.

Consider the growth of Social Security spending. For

decades Social Security was claimed to be an old age pension. Everyone would be forced to set aside a portion of his or her wages to be guaranteed a government pension to supplement a private pension or personal savings—or, in the case of those who had no other source of funds, it provided a last resort of funds. For the program to work like a real pension plan, the Social Security tax dollars would have been allowed to build up in a trust fund. Congress never let that happen. Every time money started to build up in the trust fund, Congress voted to raise Social Security payments, keeping the program barely solvent.

Now, except for a fraction of Social Security benefits that represent repayment of taxes paid in the past, most Social Security recipients are paid many times more than what they contributed. The real (inflation–adjusted) average monthly Social Security payments to retired couples increased 54% from 1970 to 1990. That is, people who received Social Security benefits in 1990 were getting much higher—54% higher—payments than those who were collecting checks in 1970. Whether or not higher Social Security payments are a good idea is not the issue. The point is that Congress decided to devote more of National Income to that purpose. **Social Security payments, like all federal programs, are politically determined and can be changed any time Congress decides to do so.**

Except for interest payments on the federal debt, Congress can increase or decrease any expenditure. Congress and the president will not admit this fact. To talk about cutting Social Security and all the other things now called entitlements is understood to be political suicide. **Politicians who want to stay in office for life are not willing to address tough spending issues, so they define them away.**

Tight Budgets?

There are consistent claims that federal spending on domestic programs has been gutted. "The politics of greed" is at fault; the Reagan administration cut the domestic budget to the bone. Let us consider the budget numbers. We start with the entire budget and subtract a few major categories, which leaves us with domestic expenditures:

> **Total Federal Expenditures**
>   **minus national defense**
>   **minus foreign aid**
>   **minus interest payments on the debt**
>   <u>**minus the savings and loan bailout**</u>
> **= Federal Domestic Expenditures**

What happened during the Reagan years to federal domestic expenditures? Inflation–adjusted domestic expenditures increased $26 billion during the Reagan years! This was less than the increase during the Carter years, but there was still a real increase in the domestic budget.

From 1977 to 1993 federal domestic expenditures, adjusted for inflation, have risen 40%. Inflation–adjusted domestic government spending rose 12% during the four Carter years (3% per year); 4% during the eight Reagan years (1/2% per year); and given the current budget, 24% during the Bush administration from 1989 to 1993 (6% per year). During the Reagan years the economy grew faster than the growth of domestic spending, so the percent of National Income devoted to domestic spending fell slightly, but total dollars devoted to domestic programs increased.

Federal government domestic spending has exploded during the early 1990s. In inflation–adjusted 1991 dollars, domestic spending was $689 billion in fiscal year 1989. It will be at least $858 billion in fiscal year 1993, an increase

of over 24% in four years. Federal domestic spending has
been growing much faster than the sluggish economy. The
share of National Income devoted to domestic spending
rose from 14.9% to 18% over the same four year period.

Where did all these extra dollars—3.1% of National
Income—come from? About half came from the fall in
defense spending. Remember stories a few years ago about
the bloated Pentagon with its $6,000 coffee pots and $200
hammers? During the Kennedy administration in the 1960s,
defense spending consumed over 10% of National Income.
That fell to 6.7% of National Income in 1990 and is falling
to 4.9% in 1995. **There was indeed a "peace dividend"
from the fall of the USSR that has allowed defense
spending to be cut. But taxpayers did not get the "peace
dividend." It was spent by Congress—twice over.**

Forgotten Cities and States?

California, Connecticut, and New Jersey are among the
many states that have enacted big tax increases recently.
The states claim to be strapped for cash. After the Los
Angeles riots in May 1992, big–city mayors and assorted
governors marched in Washington, claiming that the federal
government has cut payments to cities and states to the
bone. They claimed there might be riots nationwide if the
federal dollars did not flow.

One question not asked is why citizens in Medford,
Oregon, and Albany, Georgia, should pay taxes to the
federal government that it then sends to Los Angeles and
Atlanta? Why should citizens in Los Angeles and Atlanta
pay taxes to the federal government that it sends to Medford and Albany? **City services are most efficiently
provided and paid for at the city level, not by paying
federal bureaucrats to collect and distribute money. But
mayors and governors, like other politicians, want to be**

able to pass out goodies that are not tied to a tax bill.

Setting aside the foolishness of having federal taxes pay for local services, what has happened to federal grants to state and local governments? In the five years from 1987 to 1992, federal aid rose from $106 billion to $171 billion. Adjusting for inflation, there was a one–third increase in funding from the federal government in just five years. Because the economy grew less than 10% over that five–year period, the cities and states received a huge increase in funding. Of course it never hurts to ask for more.

Keeping pace with the spending increases at the federal level, total state and local government spending rose more than 120% during the decade of the 1980s. If we correct that increase to allow for inflation, state and local spending rose 40% in real terms during the 1980s. You can decide if your state provides 40% more in services now than you paid for a decade ago.

Spending Trends

Except for defense spending, which is dropping however it is measured, government spending on just about everything else has been rising, no matter how it is measured. When anyone claims that public programs are being short changed, ask them, "Compared to what?" Because government spending is taking a growing share of our nation's income, by definition there are fewer dollars left in the private sector of the economy. Let's get an idea of where the added dollars have been going.

State and local public employee compensation rose more than four times faster than it did for private employees in the 1980s. State government employee wages went up more than private employee wages did in 46 states. Local government employee wages went up more than private employee wages did in 49 states. If state and local government employees wages had gone up at the same rate as private sector employees wages during the 1980s, state and local governments would have saved $40 billion.

Governments are spending more money and are hiring more people. The number of federal employees fell during the first two years of the Reagan administration, but it has been upward ever since, now exceeding 3 million employees, despite military cutbacks. State governments increased the number of their employees by about 20% during the 1980s, to about 4.5 million. Local governments increased employment by 10%, to over 10 million employees.

Most large private organizations, taking advantage of efficiency–enhancing devices such as computers, and seeking greater productivity, have cut employment. During the 1980s, the number of people employed in the private sector increased by almost 20 percent. All of this gain incurred in businesses with fewer than 1,000 employees. Giant corporations did not add employees.

That governments are inefficient organizations is not the fault of government employees. Despite concern expressed about waste in government, Congress reveals no interest in allowing government agencies to modernize and take advantage of cost–saving measures. In legislation in 1991, for example, Congress prevented the Farmers Home Administration from using private collection agencies to help collect billions of dollars in defaulted loans.

Many appropriation bills prohibit federal agencies from saving money unless Congress says they can. Congress also requires many federal programs to hire a certain number of people, preventing agency managers from eliminating unnecessary staffs or contracting out for some services. **Congressional micro–management of federal agencies can force spending beyond what an agency requests; it belies the rhetoric of most politicians that they are concerned about waste in government.**

Congress Is Big Business

At the beginning of the 1900s, Congress needed fewer employees than there were members of Congress to run its operation. Now there are 50 employees for every member of Congress—over 25,000 employees to keep the machine going that decides how to spend $1.5 trillion a year. At the beginning of the 1900s, the federal government spent 2.5% of our income; now it spends 25%. Are we ten times better off than Americans in 1900?

Chapter 4

Is the American Dream Over?

One doesn't need to read the many doomsday books to know that the American economy is stagnating. America's history has been one in which each generation could expect to live better than the previous generation. This was not an illusion, for real economic growth per person in this country averaged 2% per year in this century until about 1970. Certainly, the baby–boomers growing up in the 50s and 60s knew they would live better than their parents lived in the 20s, 30s, and 40s. That was a reasonable expectation that was borne out by experience.

Today there is pessimism unknown since the Great Depression. We are much wealthier than we were in the 30s, but those who are starting out now after high school or college are finding the real world tough going. Few young people talk about being better off than their parents and their expectations are borne out by the data. In fact, many are relying on their parents to help them maintain a satisfactory standard of living as young adults. The biggest gain many young adults can hope for is an inheritance when they are middle aged.

The disillusionment expressed by young adults is not

inappropriate: our economy is stagnant. **If the economy had continued to grow at its historical rate of 2% per year (a modest rate), average income would be 50% higher today.** There would be no "lack of resources" for government programs. There would be a lot less poverty. The fruits of what little growth we have enjoyed, such as in the 80s, have been consumed by the government.

I'm Here to Help You

The ugly poverty in Eastern Europe and in the ex–Soviet Union revealed after the collapse of communism put another nail in the coffin of the idea that socialism can work or that economies can be centrally planned. Despite the lesson we have learned from the terrible experiences of those nations, we continue to move toward democratic socialism. **Under democratic socialism, elected government leaders, rather than individual citizens, decide how we spend most of our income. Despite the opposition to ever expanding government expressed by most political leaders, that growth continues with no end in sight.**

Few politicians admit to favoring tax increases (except for those to be imposed on a few rich folks). In fact, most claim they want to cut tax burdens for most citizens. At the same time, despite the rapid growth of government expenditures, we hear the same politicians say "Budgets are tight," "The states are strapped for cash," and "The Reagan years gutted social programs." These claims are used to justify higher taxes and they indicate strong political incentives to keep governments growing. **While most politicians tell voters they oppose higher taxes and big government, they vote to make them happen.**

Paid To Be Poor

Taking from Peter to pay Paul never was an economic growth strategy and it still is not. It tells Peter he does not get to keep the fruits of his labor and tells Paul he does not have to labor to get any fruits. This is the story of the "Great Society" programs started about 1965.

In the Great Society, our political leaders decided to give a lot more public assistance benefits to low income people. In 1965, at the start of the Great Society, 4.3 million people were receiving Aid to Families with Dependent Children (AFDC) benefits, the primary welfare program. Then the amount of public assistance benefits increased rapidly. Food stamps and public housing projects were started, AFDC payments increased, more medical benefits were provided, and so forth.

The Great Society kicked up the share of National Income devoted to public assistance by 158% from 1965 to 1975. During those ten years, the number of people receiving AFDC rose 162%, to 11.3 million, from 1965 to 1975. The more people are paid to be on welfare, the more people will volunteer to be on welfare. That statement is not intended to be mean. **It is a fact that when the government takes from Peter to pay Paul, more people will want to be Paul.**

Poverty is real. The best way to cure poverty is not to take from Peter to pay Paul, but to have economic opportunities for Paul. Not just conservatives who hate welfare know that economic growth is the best help for the poor; liberals like Jesse Jackson have preached that fact for years. **There must be economic growth for poverty to be eliminated, but our political leaders show no interest in making that happen. Politicians want to take from Peter to give to Paul, so that Paul will vote for them.**

Our prediction, and that of many who have studied the

data, is simple. **Unless we change what the government is doing to our economy, we will not again see the 2% per person annual growth in take–home pay that we used to take for granted.** The poverty problem and many other problems will get worse.

Gridlock

We are in economic gridlock. The slow end of the recession means that instead of experiencing actual economic decline, we will return to staying even. There is no reason to think that boom times are ahead. This generation, and even more so the next generation, are the first in American history to have no reason to expect to be wealthier than previous generations.

But there is no law of nature or economics that says our economy must be stuck. We have brought this on ourselves by allowing our political leaders to tax and regulate us into gridlock. Other economies (some wealthier than ours) continue to grow and prosper. They are not saddled with the consequences of a political system that is concerned with who gets the goodies that exist; they are encouraging more goodies to be created that all may enjoy.

We have no reason to believe that our political leaders will change the policies that have brought us to gridlock. **They have no incentive to change the structure of our government. They continue to be political winners by sticking with what we have, despite their talk about wanting change. If members of Congress really wanted reform, we would have it already.**

Stuck in the Mud

Until recently, the people of each generation could dream of having more than their parent's generation. That is no longer true. The average worker has made no real gain for over twenty years. And the multi–trillion dollar set of entitlements Congress has mandated for us, to be financed by trillions in debt we pass on to our children, threatens the next generation's hope of even matching the income of the present generation.

The average wage of American workers, inflation adjusted, is the same today as it was 25 years ago. Since taxes have risen, the inflation adjusted average take–home pay of workers is about the same as it was 30 years ago. The situation is even worse for young workers and those without a college degree. **The average wages of workers under age 30 and of workers without a college education have fallen over the past 20 years.**

Let's look at government statistics about what happened to median income, the income earned by households in the middle of the pack—the average American—over a 20–year period.

MEDIAN HOUSEHOLD INCOME
(Inflation Adjusted $)

Household	1968	1988	% Change
Under age 24	$ 20,492	$ 17,040	−17
Age 25 to 34	29,208	28,408	−3
Age 35 to 44	33,403	36,554	+9
Age 45 to 54	33,219	38,213	+15
Age 55 to 64	25,934	28,903	+11
Age 65 and up	10,810	14,923	+38
Married, wife works	36,326	42,709	+18
Married, wife not work	27,926	27,220	−3

As we discussed before, until about 1970, we had a long

history of 2% real growth per year. That meant that wages, adjusted for inflation, rose an average of 2% per year over the long haul; real income doubled each generation. Now, the only group with incomes rising in the 2% per year range are retirees. Folks over age 65 are cashing in big on the Social Security benefits passed out so generously by Congress at the expense of workers today and tomorrow. But even if we took away the increase in Social Security, and returned those tax dollars to the workers, the picture would remain bleak.

Because there has been very little economic gain for the average worker, most families now have two workers. When both spouses work, many expenses go up, such as higher clothing and food bills, child care, and the purchase of other services that were done by the housewife in Ozzie and Harriet days. Even if wives work out of choice, not just for the extra money, much of the income gain to the two worker families goes to expenses related to working, so there is little real economic gain to the family.

Why Are We Stuck?

As we will see when we look at the federal budget deficit, if the economy had continued to grow at its long–term trend the budget would be balanced today. But it is not growing at that trend. The economy does not grow, but government expenditures do. **Congress continues to spend as if we were getting wealthier and, worse yet, claims that we need more government programs to spur economic growth.**

When the economy stalls for no obvious reason that people can see, lots of possible reasons are offered. Some say the problem is that young people today do not know how to work. Perhaps they are less prepared for the labor force, but only marginally so. Young people today have the same desire to get ahead as people have always had. But because of the decline in productivity growth, young workers today are paid less for the same work than were young workers in past decades; they have to work longer and harder just to stay even.

Some say that the problem is that business leaders do not know how to compete. This is just hype. The share of National Income produced by the largest corporations is declining; our economy and the world economy are more competitive than ever. That competition, and the technological progress it produces, provides us better and cheaper goods. Competition is one of the key things that has kept our standard of living from falling.

The Regulatory Burden

Congress can spend two ways: by spending dollars or by forcing people and businesses to spend on things they might not want. Direct spending is easier to see and understand—Congress wants money so its members can give goodies to their friends. Another way to control resources is to force others to spend resources. Consider just the hours you spend doing federal income taxes, which is estimated to be 30 hours per year on average. That is regulatory spending—you spend time (and money if you hire an accountant) doing something the government requires.

The private sector incurs huge costs complying with regulation. Most of these costs have come about in the past 20 years or so. The budgets of regulatory agencies are minuscule as a share of federal spending—about 1%, but this amount is five times what it was in 1970, in inflation-adjusted dollars. So there is no question that, just like entitlements, regulatory spending has exploded in the past 20 years.

Back in the 1950s and 60s, new and revised federal regulations took less than 20,000 pages per year to print in the *Federal Register*. In the past 20 years, new and revised regulations take over 60,000 pages per year to print—a good indication of the massive increase in the regulatory burden faced by the private sector.

Every new regulation has its horror stories. Some businesses fail because the costs of complying with the regulation are so high and, of course, consumers pick up the tab. For instance, in 1992 a new Occupational Safety and Health regulation applies to 5.6 million health–care workers. It is supposed to reduce the risk of AIDS infection. Like many regulations, an elephant gun is used to shoot a mouse.

The government claims it will cost about $1 billion to comply with this regulation, but the evidence already is that the real cost will be many times higher. Most dentists and doctors will have to raise their rates between $5 and $40 per patient just to cover the costs of complying with the regulation. The Emergency Medical Services Authority in Oklahoma, which provides ambulance service for most of the state, increased its rates $38.05 per ambulance ride to cover the cost of the regulation. There is no link between costs and benefits; this is just one of the hundreds of regulations that raise costs and lower productivity. In this case the cost of health care is driven up one more time— which will probably result in Congressional hearings about why health care costs are rising.

The regulations various agencies impose—as mandated by Congress—are equivalent to a major tax. **The total cost to society of various federal regulations is now in the range of $500 billion a year, or about $5,000 for every household in America.** This cost is about the same as the entire amount paid in Social Security taxes and in personal income taxes. Because regulatory compliance is private-sector spending required by government, it is the same as if taxes had been paid to the government to perform the chores dictated by regulation.

The regulatory burden should be added to direct spending to get a better idea of the cost of government. Federal spending in 1992 is about $1.5 trillion. Add $500 billion in regulatory costs and the real federal budget increases to $2 trillion in 1992, which is 42% of National Income. To this sum, we can add state and local government spending of $825 billion. **Almost 60% of our National Income goes to direct expenditures by government and to expenditures the government forces us to make.**

Besides the cost of following regulatory orders, there is an uncounted cost from reduced productivity. When business spends money on regulatory compliance, it reduces the amount of money it has left to spend on new equipment that would increase productivity, wages, and national income. If federal regulations could be shown to benefit society, then the cost would be easy to justify. But the vast majority of studies about regulation show the costs to be greater than the benefits. Indeed, the costs are usually several times the benefits, making expenditures on regulation almost a pure waste of money.

Many regulations are anti–competitive and anti–consumer. They provide monopoly privileges to special interests that Congress rewards for campaign support. Members of Congress know this is true—they know exactly what is going on because they order the regulations to begin with and monitor the regulatory process very closely. **Congress imposes costly and anti–competitive regulations, and even regulations that do the opposite of what they are claimed to do, because the regulations benefit their friends who help them get reelected time and again.** Behind virtually every regulation is a special interest group that benefits from the regulation. The special interest group provides money, support, and votes for the reelection of members of Congress.

Breaking the Gridlock

The complex part of getting out of economic gridlock is our political gridlock. For long–term economic growth to occur, politicians must vote to reduce the tax revenues they control; they must stop passing out special privileges to special interests that do them favors; and they must stop increasing federal spending for a few years until growth occurs. Our political system does not reward politicians who keep their mitts off the dollars they have the power to grab and dole out. **We must change the incentives of our politicians or they will have no incentive to vote for policies that will allow our economy to grow and create opportunities for all people.**

Chapter 5

Where Does It All Go?

If members of Congress want to continue to occupy the marble halls of Congress (instead of live like ordinary people back home) they have to scramble for every nickel for their districts they can get. After all, Congress has decided to spend $1.5 trillion dollars; the folks back home better get a share of this if the congressional representatives want to be reelected. If the folks at home do not get a share, it will go to another state; it will not come back in a tax refund.

Pigs at the Trough

A federally funded special project is pork barrel spending, except to those who get the money—they are very grateful to the senator or representative who helped deliver the goods. That means votes and campaign contributions at election time. A list of pork barrel projects would be a hundred times the length of this book. Here are a few from 1991:

• $3.8 million for Arkansas Poultry Center of Excellence;

- $2.7 million for a fish farm in Stuttgart, Arkansas;
- $3.4 million for improvements on 5th and 6th streets in Waterloo, Iowa;
- $1 million for a performing arts center in North Miami, Florida;
- $850,000 for a bike path in Macomb County, Michigan;
- $4.5 million to renovate a theater in Huntington, West Virginia;
- $11 million for "Steamtown" in Scranton, Pennsylvania; and
- $510,000 to revitalize downtown Dayton, Washington.

Unfortunately, while such projects make good news stories, they are a drop in the bucket of federal spending. **Pork barrel projects are mere trinkets in the giant bag of goodies that Congress passes out to benefit special interests and appeal to various interests of voters—us.**

Most citizens support basic government projects and services. But the cost of providing these things are greater than need be and money is wasted on projects of little value, because senators and representatives constantly worry about how to get reelected. Catering to special interests by members of Congress is a serious problem because it distorts the structure of government spending. **Special interest politics, not working for the greater good of the nation, drives Congressional spending.**

Are Bureaucrats Out of Control?

A long-time favorite campaign line of people running for Congress is that they want to eliminate waste in government and reign in wasteful bureaucrats who are out of control. Such statements represent fine sentiments but do not square with reality. Congress is well informed about waste in government—wasteful projects are approved every

year by Congress. Members of Congress are very well
informed about what is going on in the agencies they create
and fund every year. Congress watches all federal bureaucrats closely, except for judges and some people in the
White House. Congress creates bureaucracies and gives
them detailed budgets and instructions every year. **A
bureaucrat who is truly out of control is a bureaucrat
headed for early retirement.**

The people who work for government agencies are
intelligent and conscientious; they are Americans who
happened to end up with a government job instead of a job
in the private sector. Most government employees want
their agencies to be effective; they do not sit around
plotting how to waste tax dollars.

Military Madness?

The military is just another bureaucracy, working to
provide what its top bureaucrats, called generals, think will
be most effective in military terms. The military makes its
spending request to Congress. Then what happens? Projects
that military experts claim are worthwhile, like the B–2
bomber, are slashed. Is this because Congress wants to save
dollars to return to the taxpayers? No, it wants to spend the
money on things that make other special interests happy.

For example, in 1991 the House Armed Services Committee, apparently worried that the military brass would leave
the country undefended, gave the military $1 billion *more*
than requested to fund the reserve forces, including $280
million to be spent on National Guard armories in 100
congressional districts. At a time when we are supposed to
be cutting unnecessary military spending, the Army got
$270 million for 60 more M–1 tanks than it requested,
because the Ohio and Michigan delegations lobbied for the
expenditures, which benefit tank builders in their states.

Congress authorized $2 billion in 1992 for the nuclear Seawolf submarine that the Pentagon did not want. Members of Congress from Connecticut and other states that get the money to build the submarines kept the project alive. At the same time Congress was keeping this boondoggle alive, it was wondering where to get money for urban projects after the Los Angeles riots.

Members of Congress love the cartoons that show fat, stupid generals buying $800 toilet seats, because it lets senators and representatives pretend they are guardians against military waste. In fact, it is Congress that orders such purchases. **Generals, like other bureaucrats, can be forced to spend money they did not request and that they know is for a wasteful project.**

The Nuclear Metals Company of Massachusetts lobbied successfully in 1991 to get Congress to approve $200 million to buy 36 million pounds of depleted uranium, which is used to make armor–piercing bullets. The military did not ask for it, said it did not need it, and can get all it wants for free from the Department of Energy. The push for the bill was led by Republican and Democrat senators from South Carolina and Tennessee. The reasoning behind this expenditure was clear after the company doled out $25,000 in campaign contributions in 1989 and 1990. (Not a bad investment to get $200 million.)

Similarly, a plant in North Dakota has been making jewel bearings used in watches and instruments since the 1950s. By law, the Pentagon must buy all output from the factory. The Pentagon inspector general requested cutting off purchases because there is an 84–year supply of the stuff, but Congress knows better.

Even the Best Intentions...

Many programs start off with decent intentions, but by

definition create a special interest that keeps lobbying for more and more, long after the initial project was completed. Decades ago, Congress created the Rural Electrification Administration (REA) to help bring electricity to farmers and small towns in America. Since that work was pretty well completed by the 1940s, Congress told the REA to string telephone wires, too. That's all finished too. You will have to look long and hard to find people who do not have electricity or telephone service.

But the REA continues to make taxpayer–subsidized loans at below–market interest rates. For example, Dell Telephone Co–op in rural West Texas has borrowed $14 million to construct a phone system for 772 customers ($18,000 per head). Dell pays the REA interest rates of 2% and 5% on this money, investing almost half the money at far higher interest rates. The REA admits Dell could give phone service away because it makes such high profits off the money it borrows cheap and lends dear. Little Dell is not alone on the gravy train; major companies get on too. Big GTE Corporation borrowed $42 million at 5% interest for a Micronesian subsidiary in the South Pacific. (By the way, Congress has declared the REA program to be an "entitlement.")

The List Keeps Growing

Remember the $200 billion–plus catastrophe called the savings and loan bailout? That happened because of government policies that encouraged high–risk loans, all backed by the full faith and credit of the U.S. taxpayers. Despite the pious finger–pointing in Congress and within the administration over that mess, has there been a move to prevent similar happenings? Of course not. The U.S. government (taxpayers) backs hundreds of billions of dollars worth of loans to countries around the world that do not have a hope of ever repaying the money.

Agriculture is also riddled with wasteful programs. Americans pay double the world price for sugar, adding over $3 billion a year to our grocery bills, according to the U.S. Department of Commerce. This keeps a few sugar farmers in business in the U.S. who would otherwise do something else. It also means that poor sugar growers in the Philippines, Haiti, and other places are denied the chance to earn a living by selling their goods to the U.S. (Then Congress sends those countries foreign aid because it is supposedly worried about how poor their people are.)

Who benefits from this extra $30–a–year–per–family sugar bill in the U.S.? **One Florida family alone provides 15% of the cane sugar in the country. Sugar price protection earns the family an extra $50 to $90 million a year!** The family is very grateful to politicians for this. The family gave Mr. Bush $100,000 in 1988 to support his presidential campaign. But President Bush was not alone; the family made 141 contributions, totalling $287,000, in 1988 to assorted Republicans and Democrats around the country. Like the other sugar growers that provide campaign contributions through PACs, this family gets a very handsome return on its investment in campaigns.

In 1990 the Senate voted to keep the sugar subsidies in place by a vote of 54–44. According to the Center for Public Integrity, senators who received no contributions from the sugar industry all voted against the subsidy. Almost all senators who received $15,000 or more in contributions voted for the subsidy. **Congress and the administration are induced by a couple million bucks a year in campaign contributions to keep programs going that the government admits costs consumers billions of dollars a year.**

Wasting money on rich sugar farmers may be foolish, but it pales in comparison to handing out $5 billion in loans

guaranteed by the full faith and credit of the U.S. government (that is, American taxpayers) to Saddam Hussein in
Iraq in the years right before the Gulf War. Why was this
done? Members of Congress from farm states wanted to
subsidize grain sales to Iraq, so clever people in the State
Department advised the Reagan and Bush folks that we
could buy Iraq's friendship. Everyone now knows that the
deal in Iraq was bad. But are all the other handouts to other
countries around the world any more sensible?

Government and R&D

Some politicians claim that the government should do
more for research and development. After all, innovations
are important to advances in productivity and our standard
of living. The problem is that government R&D spending
is determined by the same system that gives us high–priced
sugar and stockpiles of depleted uranium and useless
jewels.

Consider the high–tech space agency NASA. Congress
treats it like any other government program. Politics
dominates decisions. In the 1991 budget, Congress tacked
on $100 million for projects *never requested* by NASA.
Senator Byrd from West Virginia, a senior and powerful
member of the Senate, got $22.5 million for a National
Technology Transfer Center in Morgantown, West Virginia,
and $7.5 million for a Jesuit college in Wheeling, West
Virginia. There was also $20 million for the Christopher
Columbus Center for Marine (not space) Research in
Baltimore, and so forth. **It does not matter if the subject
is defense, agriculture, or research—program decisions
are dominated by special interests, not by concern about
how to try to make effective use of resources.**

The list of wasteful spending is so long and the amounts
of money so large that we become immune to discussions

about them. Members of Congress know these projects are not worthwhile, but to get a share for their respective states, each has to go along. Every senator and representative can truthfully claim that he or she opposes many wasteful projects; but they all hop on the wagon when their special interests are at stake. The nature of our political system is such that we, the voters, demand that our politicians fight for our share. **The federal budget is loaded with billions of dollars worth of economically senseless projects. But, even if these were all wiped out, we would not have solved the spending problem.**

Where the Big Bucks Flow

In Chapter 3 we defined federal domestic spending as the federal budget minus the amounts spent on defense, foreign aid, interest on the debt, and the savings and loan bailout. As the table shows, domestic spending by the federal government has risen rapidly for several decades. In constant (inflation adjusted) dollars, it is eight times greater than it was 40 years ago.

DOMESTIC SPENDING
($ Billion)

Year	Current $	Constant (1991) $
1953	$ 16.04	$ 105.75
1963	45.37	210.54
1973	147.68	439.27
1983	496.26	666.24
1993	913.91	858.05

Most of the big growth in domestic federal spending in

recent years has been in Social Security, Medicare, and Medicaid, which we will call SSM&M. In the next table, we break down federal domestic spending in constant (inflation–adjusted) 1991 dollars into two parts: one part is SSM&M; the other part is all other federal domestic spending.

In the 20 years from 1973 to 1993, inflation–adjusted spending on all federal domestic programs except SSM&M rose 46%, but spending on SSM&M rose 164%. The explosive growth of SSM&M is not expected to end anytime soon. SSM&M now takes 10% of National Income now and will take over 12% of National Income by the year 2000.

FEDERAL DOMESTIC SPENDING
(Constant 1991 $ Billions)

Year	SSM&M	All Other
1953	$ 17.93	$ 87.82
1963	74.01	136.52
1973	183.65	255.63
1983	325.29	340.95
1993	484.45	373.60

How did this happen? Congress, with the blessing of several presidents, has consistently voted for more and more benefits for those eligible for SSM&M. The result has been an explosion of spending on these programs. The benefits received are many times more than the taxes contributed. **The gifts that have been passed out to people now or soon eligible for Social Security, Medicare, and Medicaid are really no different than welfare payments or food stamps.**

Demand Your Share Now

Every taxpayer is forced to pay for benefits that go to a host of special interest groups. At the same time, we are all members of special interest groups that want benefits from government. Because we pay a large share of our income to the government, we want our representatives to give us something back. We cannot volunteer to do without federal benefits in exchange for a cut in our taxes. **If we do not demand our share of the goodies passed out by Congress that we help pay for, they will go elsewhere.**

The economic problem is that, compared to private decisions to spend money and produce goods and services, production and consumption decisions by government are, like any socialist–style planning, inefficient. Compound that with the incentives of politicians to make special interests happy and the inefficiency of government programs is made even worse. We get a few cents worth of benefit for every dollar spent or, as in cases like stockpiling depleted uranium or giving money to Saddam Hussein, there are no benefits; we may as well have burned the dollars.

Seniority and experience in Congress means more goodies for the folks back home. Suppose the voters in one state said "Enough!" and sent people to Washington who voted against all federal spending and refused to take any federal benefits for their state. Would the senators and representatives from the other 49 states reward that state with a lower federal tax bill? Of course not. They would happily strip the taxpayers of that state bare, providing a few more goodies for their own folks back home. **The structure of the political system makes it sensible for voters to return their senators and representatives to Washington time and again, in order to get their share of the federal pie. To do otherwise would be irrational and useless under the current system.**

Chapter 6

The Deficit and the Debt

The federal government budget deficit for 1992 may hit $400 billion. The 1992 deficit—the amount of spending above tax revenues in one year—is as much as Americans paid in total income taxes to the federal government *in 1988*. The deficit means the government spent $1,500 more than it had in tax revenues for every person—including babies and senior citizens—in the country. **We need $300 more in taxes every month from *every worker* in America just to balance the budget. Americans are paying $500 billion in income taxes in 1992, but every taxpayer would have to pay 80% more in income taxes just to balance the budget.**

The amount borrowed by the federal government in 1992 to finance the deficit took 8% of our National Income. It is about the same amount of money as Americans spent on automobiles, appliances, furniture, computers, and other things we call durable goods. It is about the same amount of money as all businesses in the country invested in "durable equipment"—new machinery, computers, and other things that make our economy grow. It is double the total income of the agricultural sector of the country. It is a *lot* of money.

Regardless of opinions about how high federal taxes and spending should be, just about everyone agrees the deficit is too big. Some politicians say that some taxes should be raised to help reduce the deficit; others say that some spending should be cut to reduce the deficit. Whatever the talk, there has obviously been no real intention to deal with the matter. The massive deficit has been building for years. Everyone in Washington understands the problem, but few have the political courage to deal with it.

Hike Taxes to Balance the Budget?

To reduce the deficit, spending must be cut or taxes increased. A massive tax increase would make the problem worse because it would reduce economic growth, which would keep future tax revenues down. More importantly, the voters will not tolerate a massive tax increase. We are soon likely to see a tax hike on "the rich," but this will not balance the budget. The revenues will not be enough to cover a fraction of the deficit—even if Congress did not use the new revenues for more new spending, which is what they are most likely to do.

A 1991 study prepared for the Joint Economic Committee of Congress found that **since 1947 higher taxes have always led to higher deficits: every new dollar of tax revenues resulted in $1.59 in new spending.** This is not the case at the state level. Since 1947, every new dollar of tax revenues resulted in 93 cents in new spending.

Most states have balanced budget requirements in their constitutions that prevent state legislators from incurring perpetual deficits that are supposedly beyond control. While balanced budget requirements help, politicians get around them by going "off-budget" for many projects. They set up "corporations" that can incur debt. The states also issue bonds to finance various projects, but they avoid calling this deficit spending. **Although balanced–budget requirements are not perfect, they do impose some fiscal responsibility on state governments.**

Cut Spending to Balance the Budget?

As we saw in the last chapter, the growth of federal spending has been much faster than the growth of the economy. If domestic spending had been held to the same share of National Income it was ten years ago, the budget would be balanced. In fact, most of the deficit would be eliminated if domestic spending had been held to the levels it was at in the late 1980s.

Most of the deficit is due to the high growth of domestic spending during the past couple years. If domestic spending had increased every year at the same rate as inflation, the deficit would be quite small. Federal spending does not have to actually be cut to move toward a balanced budget. We would be near a balanced budget today if federal spending had grown at the same rate as the rest of the economy.

Congress and the Bush administration could not stand it. There were no new goodies to pass out—just the same old trillion dollars worth of stuff in the budget. There was no new clever federal program like the "War on Poverty," which has spent over $2 trillion since 1965. There was nothing new to hand out to special interests.

Budget Busting

The Gramm–Rudman–Hollings Deficit Reduction Act of 1985 set fixed deficit targets for the future that would gradually move the federal government to a balanced budget. That act said, basically, that federal spending would go up at the rate of inflation, which is about what was happening then. Congress and the administration could fight over how to spend the dollars on hand, but spending was to stay within the agreed budget limits. This resulted in a falling deficit every year up to 1989.

In the six years from 1983 through 1988, the economy grew at an average rate of 4% per year. Our nation's real (inflation adjusted) income went up 25% during those years. Federal domestic spending grew a little faster than the rate of inflation—but not as fast as average personal income went up. Apparently the Bush administration and Congress thought they could make better decisions with our money than we can, so they delivered a tax hike, a big boost in federal domestic spending, a recession, and a deficit that rose from $115 billion to $400 billion in three years.

Any act Congress passes, it can repeal. That is what the Bush administration and Congress did with the "historic" budget agreement with a tough–guy name, the Budget Enforcement Act of 1990. Because Congress did not want to outright ignore Gramm–Rudman, which might have presented legal problems, they dumped it. Everyone knew from the start that the new agreement was a farce that could never deliver a balanced budget. The 1990 agreement set much higher "limits" on domestic spending than Gramm–Rudman allowed. Even these higher "limits" were quickly exceeded. The 1990 bi–partisan agreement pretended that tax revenues would be much higher than they could possibly be, which allowed the act to pretend that the budget would be balanced.

The president's budget people in the Office of Management and Budget (OMB) claimed in 1990 that the new budget law would produce a deficit about half of what it turned out to be in 1992 and that the budget would be in *surplus* by 1994. Every few months since the 1990 agreement, OMB and the Congressional Budget Office trot out revised estimates. They show two things: Spending has

gone up more than was agreed upon and tax revenues have
not come in as fast as was predicted. The result has been
giant deficits.

The Bush administration blames Congress for not living
up to the budget agreement. There is truth in that claim, but
the agreement actually allowed much higher spending;
everyone knew the future tax revenue estimates were a
fiction; and Mr. Bush broke his clear campaign promise not
to raise taxes. Members of Congress blame everyone,
including Congress. Many crocodile tears are shed, but
Congress goes right on voting for higher spending. Obviously, the Democrats have no political reason to help Mr.
Bush get the budget mess straightened out. **Senators and
representatives do not have the will or the incentive to
deal with the deficit—it means telling too many sup-
porters they cannot have the goodies they want.**

Good News, Bad News

The good news is that the doomsayers are wrong; we are
not headed down the economic drain—at least not very fast.
In fact, the deficit might drop a bit over the next couple
years; military spending is falling, the savings and loan
bailout, which cost $80 billion in 1992, will be winding
down, and, presumably, the economy will pull out of the
recession so tax revenues will rise.

The bad news is that nothing has changed. Special
interests, whether Social Security check collectors, city
mayors, farmers on subsidies, and a host of others, continue
to pressure Congress and the White House for more
benefits. **The result is that each of us still thinks the
same way: A dollar that is now in someone else's pocket
would look better in mine; the member of Congress who
gets it for me will be most appreciated.**

Balanced Budget Amendment?

There has always been widespread popular support for a balanced budget. Polls consistently show that over two–thirds of the citizens favor a balanced budget amendment to the Constitution. The framers of the Constitution did not include a balanced budget requirement because they never imagined the massive federal government that would begin to grow 150 years later and that would run deficit after deficit 200 years later.

Citizens may disagree about how much we should spend and who should pay for it, but most agree that, except for emergencies like war, the federal budget should be balanced. Reflecting that support, over thirty state legislatures have passed a resolution calling for a constitutional convention to draft a balanced budget amendment for the Constitution.

Only a few more states are needed to force a constitutional convention (two–thirds must call for a convention). Congress and special interest groups are scared that the two–thirds vote may be reached and have been lobbying hard in state legislatures to stop the movement. The convention would be likely to adopt a tougher amendment than Congress would like to see. Most members of Congress claim they want a balanced budget, but their failure to force themselves to adopt one shows that there is no desire to have their spending habits restricted. As the director of the Congressional Budget Office said, **"The deficit cannot be brought down without making painful decisions to cut specific programs and raise particular taxes."**

The balanced budget amendment most commonly pushed by those who are serious about the issue says the following:

1. Each year the president must present a balanced budget

to Congress—must show that revenues match expenditures.

2. Congress then works on the budget to its satisfaction. A budget that has a deficit can be approved only by sixty percent of the members of the Senate and of the House, on a roll call vote—name by name.

3. The balanced budget requirement can be waived when a declaration of war is in effect.

4. Votes for any new taxes or increase in the national debt must be approved by a sixty percent vote of the members of both houses on a roll call vote.

Such an amendment missed getting two–thirds of the votes in the Senate by one vote in 1986, fell seven votes shy of two–thirds in the House in 1990, and fell nine votes shy of two–thirds in the House in June of 1992. Supposedly, members of Congress were worried that 1992 is an election year in which the voters are going to punish those who behave irresponsibly. So some thought the balanced budget amendment was going to pass to try to make the voters happy. **Members of Congress know better: it is business as usual. To get reelected they have to keep the favors coming, not cut them off.**

Nevertheless, it is not politically wise to be against a balanced budget, so those who vote against it give many reasons why they oppose an amendment. Some claim there is no reason for an amendment—they say that Congress should just balance the budget without any constitutional requirement and they will be the first one to vote for such fiscal sanity. Congressman Jack Brooks of Texas, who has been in Washingtion since 1952, said that he knows the people are "fed up" but he voted against the amendment because it would only lead to "another round of games and charades."

Others member of Congress say they favor some other

version, that the one being voted on is not quite right. They know very well that the "perfect" version they want will never happen, so their explanation is just a sham. **By having various versions of an amendment running around, members of Congress can claim they do back an amendment; it is the fault of the rest of the members that their favorite one has not been adopted.**

Don't Touch My Goodies

Who opposes the balanced budget amendment? The biggest special interest groups—labor unions such as the AFL–CIO; big business groups such as the U.S. Chamber of Commerce; the American Association of Retired Persons that claims to represent the elderly who receive Social Security and Medicare benefits; farmers who get subsidies; and veterans who are afraid their benefits will be cut—all oppose it. **Most people are fiscal conservatives until their own special interest benefits are at stake.**

The House failed to pass the balanced budget amendment in 1992 by a vote of 280–152 for the measure (9 votes short of the 2/3 majority needed). Republicans voted 164–2 for the amendment; the Democrats opposed it 150–116. But this is not just a partisan issue. A major reason for Republican support for the amendment is that they have little power in Congress—Democrats run the show. Because Republicans have little control over the goodie bag, they are opposed to what is going on—but if the Republicans controlled Congress they might not be so happy to limit their spending.

Remember the bounced check scandal in the House? Who do you think *most opposed* the balanced budget amendment? Big check bouncers. Democrats in the House who bounced 50 or more checks voted 41–20 (67% to 33%) *against* the amendment. If the big check bouncers had not voted, the amendment would have *passed* 70% to 30%.

It is not just that those who cannot balance their own checkbook cannot balance the federal checkbook—it is all part of the arrogance of power. The outrage the voters express against the big check bouncers is right—it is all part of the attitude of being above it all and unaccountable. **Congress will oppose a balanced budget amendment as long as its members get to come back year after year to control handing out the goodies.**

Chapter 7

The Public Debt Albatross

Economists like to argue about whether or not deficits and the national debt matter. Some claim that the national debt is just like a mortgage on a house. That is, people borrow money to get a house, then pay it back over the years. Such debt is perfectly sensible and represents an investment for the future that will be repaid. But, the government is not like a private borrower who must repay debt or be forced into bankruptcy.

No one can limit the borrowing of the federal government. No one can deny the federal government a loan because it is a bad credit risk with too much debt. **The government, by acts of Congress, decides how much money to tax and spend, how much to borrow, and how much money to print.**

Investing in Ourselves

The government does not borrow money to build things like houses, which have market value in case of default on the mortgage. Almost all federal spending goes for current consumption—welfare, farm subsidies, Social Security, foreign aid, health care, defense, and the like. That does not mean these things do not have value. But the value is in the *consumption* of these things today. The amount spent on capital goods such as highways and buildings, which provide benefits for many years, is a tiny fraction of federal spending. **When politicians talk about government spending as an investment in the future, they are talking about future votes for themselves in the next election, not real investments in capital that will benefit the next generation.**

Defenders of government deficits claim that we incur deficits because as a nation we are investing in the future. In a dream world of perfect government run by angels who are not influenced by politics and who magically know what is good for everyone, the idea that government can sensibly plan for future debt repayments might make sense. But our government (and every other one) is run by ordinary people who must respond to political interests.

Aside from the problem of political interests, there is the fact that government leaders cannot know how to plan economic development that will produce future economic growth. Centrally planned economies are disasters. That is not to say that decision makers who make plans in the private sector are perfect. Private planners make mistakes. People and corporations go bankrupt; but because the deals they make are voluntary and happen in a competitive world, they cannot force all of us to pay the bills for their mistakes. Governments can. Russians, Ukrainians, Poles, and many other people live a life of poverty that will take decades to overcome because their past government leaders made all economic planning decisions. **Central economic planners in Communist nations are no better or worse than economic planners who run democratically elected governments.**

Polls indicate that most Americans think deficit spending and a huge national debt are not beneficial. Most would

probably agree with Alan Greenspan, Chairman of the
Federal Reserve System, that

> ...large and persistent deficits are slowly but inex-
> orably damaging the economy....deficits tend to pull
> resources away from net private investment...[which]
> has reduced the rate of growth of the nation's capital
> stock. This, in turn has meant less capital per work-
> er...and this will surely engender a shortfall in labor
> productivity growth and...in growth of the standard of
> living.

Savings and Productivity

The U.S. saving rate averaged about 9% from 1950 until
the late 1970s. It has been generally falling since then,
averaging less than 3% since 1986. The amount of capital
invested per worker, which comes from saving, has been
dropping too. That is a key reason why growth in labor
productivity, the output per worker, has slowed. Labor
productivity grew over 3% a year on average from World
War II until 1973; it has grown 0.9% per year since 1973.

The only way our standard of living can increase is for
labor productivity to rise. Higher productivity means more
value per worker, which means higher wages. Real economic growth comes from investment in new capital—
machines, buildings, computers, and so forth—and from
having a more skilled labor force. Growth does not come
from higher levels of government spending and debt. Before
1973, when worker productivity was increasing, capital per
worker grew at about 2.5% per year. Since 1973, capital per
worker has increased only 0.8% per year.

The slowdown in worker productivity, which is largely
attributable to the decline in investment in new capital,
means that wage gains have slowed too. From 1959 to

1973, when labor productivity grew at an average annual rate of 2.8%, real (inflation–adjusted) hourly worker pay rose 2.9% per year. Since 1973, real hourly worker pay has been rising 0.7% per year, which is consistent with the slow growth in new capital per worker and the slow growth in worker productivity.

Saving by Americans have declined because there is less reason to save and there is less ability to save. For now, let's look at the personal saving that Americans have been setting aside, and consider how much of that must be borrowed by the federal government to cover the deficit.

PERSONAL SAVING AND FEDERAL DEFICIT

Year	Saving ($ billion)	Deficit ($ billion)	Deficit/Saving (%)
1962	$ 26	$ 7.1	27.3
1972	60	23.4	39.0
1982	200	128.0	64.0
1992 (est)	240	400.0	166.7

For almost a decade, the budget deficit—the amount borrowed by the federal government to pay for spending today—has been about as much as Americans save. That is why Mr. Greenspan says the ability of the private sector to grow is being reduced. Massive borrowing by the government in the world drives up interest rates, making capital more costly in the private sector. As investment in the private sector grows more slowly, productivity and workers' wages grow more slowly. A lack of economic growth causes people to press the government for more benefits.

It is a vicious circle. More government borrowing and spending squeezes the private sector harder. The slower

the economy grows, the slower tax revenues grow. Fortunately, Europeans, Saudis, Japanese, and others have been sending some of their savings to the U.S., buying our government debt and helping provide some money for the private sector. Capital has been made available, but at a higher price than it would be without the big deficits.

Why have the Japanese and German economies kept growing? Because their rates of growth in private saving, capital investment, and, therefore, worker productivity and wages have stayed up while America's has fallen. **More government spending is not going to increase worker productivity. We face a hard economic problem, not easily resolved, that will require solutions that the current crop of participants in our political system know will be personal political suicide.**

Stealing from Children

Suppose you have a choice between two candidates for office. Candidate One says "Elect me and I will give you a pile of goodies for the taxes you now pay." Candidate Two says "Elect me and I will give you that pile of goodies—and more—for the taxes you now pay." Obviously Candidate Two is offering a better deal and, amazingly enough, may be telling the truth.

In recent years, our political leaders have learned that there are rewards in votes for being Candidate Two. Now and then they sneak in tax hikes, but mostly they deliver more goodies and do not give us a tax bill. The cost is just added to the national debt. Because they get reelected doing this, tisk–tisking about the debt all the while, they have every incentive to keep doing the same thing. **We are sticking our children and our children's children with the bill for the government benefits we are consuming today.**

The national debt is the sum of all past annual deficits in the federal budget added together. Historically, deficits were incurred in war time and then were repaid with budget surpluses. For some reason, the past few decades marked a change in behavior. Unlike the previous 180 years of the Republic, the past 20 years have seen persistent deficits.

Because the federal budget was nearly in balance until the 1970s, because the economy was growing rapidly, the debt shrank relative to National Income (NI). Consider the following table showing the federal debt compared to National Income.

FEDERAL DEBT AND NATIONAL INCOME (NI)

Year	Debt ($ billion)	NI ($ billion)	Debt/NI (%)
1950	$ 256.9	$ 220.4	116.6
1960	290.5	425.7	68.2
1970	380.9	833.5	45.7
1980	908.5	2,198.2	41.3
1990	3,206.3	4,459.6	71.9
1993 (est)	4,600.0	5,092.0	90.3

The recent growth in government expenditures is being financed in large part by deficit spending—passing much of the cost of spending today on to future generations. This generation should not complain about helping to pay the bill for having been saved from the Nazis in World War II. But should our children thank us for treating ourselves to consumption expenditures we now enjoy? **Deficit government spending today is not investing in the future, it is stealing our children's future income.**

Although the deficits are not healthful for the economy,

they are not driving us to ruin. **We do not face a financial catastrophe as some prophets of doom like to predict (for a profit).** The deficits and public debt just mean our economy grows a little more slowly than it would otherwise. We can keep adding to the pile of debt and not sink. The big deficit means that the federal government spends over $200 billion a year now in interest just to keep the federal debt rolling along; 1 of every 7 dollars in the budget is needed just for that.

The faster the debt grows, the more of the federal budget that will be devoted to paying the interest on the debt. **The federal debt is like a mortgage payment in reverse—it grows and grows, because the amount due grows and grows. Private lenders can force borrowers to make payments on their debts; no one can force the federal government to control its debt habits.**

Grand Larceny

Some retired folks put bumper stickers on their travel van that say, "We Are Spending Our Kids' Inheritance." What they probably do not know is that *they are*, as a group, spending their kids' *income*, too. Everyone knows about the official deficit and official national debt. What is discussed much less, and is an economic nightmare for the kids to inherit, is the unofficial national debt that exists because of the Social Security system.

As we discussed before, rather than let the Social Security trust fund build up so that some of the dollars we pay in Social Security taxes today are invested for payout when we retire, Congress has looted the kitty and runs the system on a pay–as–you–go basis. What does this mean for the future?

According to the former chief actuary of the Social Security Administration, Heaworth Robertson:

> The total accrued liability as of January 1, 1990,
> under Social Security...is some $12,200 billion, or
> about $12 trillion. The total assets of the Social
> Security trust funds are only $288 billion, thus the
> *unfunded* accrued liability is also approximately $12
> trillion.

That is, if Social Security, Medicare, and Medicaid
(SSM&M) were a real pension fund, it would need over
$12 *trillion* dollars in the bank *today* to cover promised
SSM&M benefits at current rates. This is a sum equal to
two years GDP or over $100,000 per worker. Obviously,
that money is not there.

When a pension company has a large unfunded liability,
we call it bankrupt. The government investigates to look for
evidence of criminal wrongdoing by the managers of the
pension funds—what happened to the money they were
supposed to have saved? But we have encouraged our
senators and representatives to legally loot the Social
Security trust fund. We reelect the members of Congress
who give us more benefits today, rather than make us save
for the future. Let the kids fend for themselves. **Politicians
who want to stay in office cannot deal with the Social
Security problem because that would require them to
tell us that there are higher taxes to be paid or lower
benefits to be distributed.**

Obviously there is no way to collect $12 trillion to make
the SSM&M system solvent. The best we can hope for is
to muddle along with the current system of benefits. Lower
benefits or higher taxes are coming some day because the
average age of our population is going up. More retirees
will be collecting benefits paid for by fewer workers. In the
1990s there are 2.2 Americans aged 35–54, the peak
earning years, for every American age 65 and over. In the
2030s, just a generation away, there will be only 1.2

Americans aged 35–54 for every one age 65 and over.

Unless there is a big unexpected change in our population—unless we start having a lot more children in a hurry or let a lot more working–age immigrants enter the country—in the future there will not be as many workers as there are now to pay Social Security taxes to cover the benefits. So taxes must go up or benefits go down.

How We Got Where We Are

How did we get into this fix? Members of Congress have consistently raided the Social Security trust fund. They started doing it in the 1950s and have not stopped. Just as the trust fund would start to build up cash to allow benefits in decades ahead to be paid, they would increase benefits for recipients today. People retired now get a lot more benefits out of the SSM&M system than they put into it.

Because of the political rhetoric of Social Security, most people who receive those benefits have no clue that they are receiving what we would ordinarily call welfare. They are told that they "earned" Social Security and have a "right" to the SSM&M benefits. A few years ago, in an honest effort to make Medicare more financially stable, Congress passed a bill to raise the premiums paid by Medicare users to cover a bigger fraction of Medicare benefits. Congress repealed the law a year later because Medicare recipients were outraged by the price hike. They threatened to throw out of office those who would force them to pay for a larger share of the benefits they receive.

Most retired people who receive such benefits are fiscal conservatives. Most probably believe welfare is for a few truly needy people. Most of these people worked hard and planned for their retirement. They were never told they would be on the welfare gravy–train. Politicians dare not tell Medicare users that they are welfare recipients—they

are getting something *they did not pay for* and do not
"deserve." **Politicians who want to stay in office cannot
deal with the Medicare and Medicaid problem. It means
telling us there are higher taxes to be paid or lower
benefits to be received.**

What do we face to keep the SSM&M system going? In
1991, we paid Social Security and Medicaid taxes of
15.51% on wages. That is, on an income of $50,000, this
tax took $7,755. Politicians long ago invented the fiction
that the employer "pays half" of these taxes. That is
nonsense—Social Security taxes are a part of the wage bill
of hiring an employee. Since employers know they have to
pay half the tax, that fact is built into wage costs. Hence,
employees really pay virtually the whole tax. But this tax
rate is just enough to keep the system afloat today. In later
years, as the number of retirees goes up compared to the
number of workers, this level of tax will not be enough.

Bleak Future

The former chief actuary of the Social Security Administration estimates that the Social Security and Medicare
tax rate will have to rise to 25% of wages by the 2030s to
keep the current system going year–by–year. The $12
trillion "deficit" is not being paid; this is what will be
needed just to keep the same level of benefits flowing. To
keep taxes at current levels, benefits will have to be cut
substantially. **Our children and young adults face a
difficult future because our political leaders gave away
too many goodies to a special interest group—everyone
now over age 50.**

Assuming we keep the same level of benefits in place,
the average 25–year–old couple today can expect, during
their working life, to pay more than three times in Social
Security and Medicare taxes than the value of benefits they

will receive at retirement age. In 40 years can the young couples turn around and treat the next generation the same way? Probably not. A 25% payroll tax, which comes before all other federal, state and local taxes, will be hard to swallow; an even higher one might spark a real tax revolt.

There is no reason to think there can be a happy ending to this story. The deficit and the debts we face are real problems that are not easy to resolve. The sooner our political leaders face the problems and start to make some hard decisions, the smaller the consequences for the next generation. But there is no politician on the national scene who dares address these issues. After all, children don't vote.

Chapter 8

The Same Old Song

How is it that a miserable barren island like Hong Kong can prosper? At the same time, some resource–rich countries like Argentina, once one of the richest countries in the world, have become poorer. **The reason is that, much like America today, they became obsessed with taking from each other through the political process, instead of encouraging everyone to work for general economic achievement.** Government policy determines if there are incentives to invest and work hard. Every politician claims to want to get America moving, but political actions usually take us in the opposite direction.

Japan and Germany do not grow because their managers know secrets that American managers do not; they grow because their saving and investment rates are much higher. There is no economic law that says that Japan will prosper because its time has come. Japan, Germany, Switzerland, Singapore, and other countries around the world grow rapidly because their governments do not discourage saving and do not punish investment.

Worrying about successful countries like Japan is the same misguided thinking that causes people to imply that some people are poor because other people are rich. During the Depression, the demagogue Huey Long wanted a law to limit anyone's income to $1 million a year. The implication was that the rich got rich by making others poor. Had that law gone into effect, the rich would have been made less rich and the poor would have been made even poorer.

The Japanese economy grows faster than ours because the Japanese are saving, investing, and producing. They make the whole world wealthier. Claiming that up–and–coming countries like Mexico hurt Americans is like saying that someone is hurt if their next–door neighbor works hard and earns a big pay raise. We may be envious of such success, but only a mean person would want to take away others' opportunity to work hard and be rewarded for their efforts. **The success of others does not come at our expense.**

Political Exploitation of Slow Growth

Americans are unhappy about the stagnant economy and the prospects of little or no economic growth in the future. Opinion poll after opinion poll point to pessimism about our economic situation. As with any nationwide concern, politicians cater to the public by claiming that "government" should and can do something about the problem.

Every candidate in the 1992 presidential primaries showed great concern over the need to "get this country moving again." Bush and Clinton offered programs for getting America going again. Being good politicians they knew what the public wanted to hear: They could run the government in a way that would get America going again.

In all fairness, all candidates talk some about the need to get the government out of the way of private economic expansion. Bush even imposed a moratorium on some new federal government regulations. But let us consider the tone and essence of the key proposals in vogue these days to get America moving:

1. Tax the rich: This proposal emanates mostly from Clinton's camp. But Bush increased taxes on the rich in 1990 and can be guaranteed to do so again if reelected. Clinton (and Perot) suggested making elderly rich people pay more taxes on their Social Security benefits.

After the Reagan *tax cuts* in the 80s, *tax revenues* from the top 1% of income earners *more than doubled*. Indeed, the top 1% of income earners paid the entire increase in federal personal income taxes during the 1980s. Cutting tax rates reduced the benefits from avoiding and evading taxes while increasing the benefits from working, earning, and investing more. The result is more work, more investment, and more tax revenues. **Making Peter pay Paul does not make the two of them wealthier.**

Interestingly, during the primaries, Jerry Brown was laughed off the podium (by the press) every time he suggested a flat tax, which is actually a serious suggestion for those who truly want to get America going again.

2. Getting the presidents of major corporations together: One of Perot's ideas about getting America going again was to involve the heads of the biggest corporations. They should meet in Washington, D.C., he said, to put their heads together to get this nation on the right track. It may be true that presidents of companies know how to run their own businesses, but they have no special competence in running the nation. Indeed, that is the point—*no one* has any special competence in running the nation.

Neither the heads of America's greatest corporations, nor the heads of any presidential administration, nor the heads of Congress have any special competence in managing a $6.5 trillion economy with 120 million workers, 15 million businesses, and 250 million consumers all engaged in billions of transactions every day.

If there is anything we learned from the disaster in the former Soviet Union, Poland, North Korea, Vietnam, Cuba, mainland China, and other centrally planned economies (or even semi-planned economies like India) it is that they do not work.

3. Let's all pull together: All presidential candidates are fond of asking the American public to "pull together" to "get this country moving again," or in the often quoted words of President Kennedy, "Ask not what your country can do for you; ask what you can do for your country." Kennedy was off the mark; what he should have said was: **Ask not what your country can do for you *or* what you can do for your country. Do what is best for you and your family and the rest will take care of itself.** While this is the old–fashioned idea of Adam Smith, who wrote it in a different form in 1776, it is now more respected since the fall of communism.

Americans do not have to be exhorted to pull together and help each other out. They do not need to be told by presidential candidates that they have to sacrifice for the good of the country. The natural state of people is a combination of competition and cooperation. The cooperation occurs naturally as we work for each other and do business with each other. We do not need to plan how we can cooperate with each other. That automatically happens in the process of living our lives; it happens in the most primitive societies and in the most complicated.

Even people who do not like the idea of individual action must admit that asking people to make sacrifices, except perhaps in time of war, never gets very far. Look at what is happening after the reunification of East and West Germany. The former West Germans are angry and have gone on strike over the relatively small sacrifices they have to make to help their poor brethren who used to live in East Germany. And this is in a country—West Germany—that has a much higher rate of economic growth than the U.S. and that is joyful over the reunification of the country.

Given the tax burdens we bear already, can you imagine what would happen in this country if we were asked to make more sacrifices than we do already for "the good of the country," for "the poor," and for the other vague things about which we tire of hearing? Who wants more of the same? The time we spend listening to politicians asking us to do more for the country—that is, to give them more power—is a high enough price to pay in itself.

4. More government commissions: Any time there is a big problem, one technique the government uses to seek a solution (or paper over the problem) is to start a commission. We have had government commissions on everything imaginable: increasing productivity, reducing waste in government, why the price of oil went up, Watergate, POW/MIAs in Vietnam, and who killed President Kennedy. The effective result of every single one of these government commissions is trivial or nothing.

Imagine the logic behind a presidential commission on increasing productivity. A group of unpaid "high-level" people sit around discussing ways to increase productivity. At the same time, most people are making a living in the real world, which means they must constantly work to increase productivity. If the people on the commission come up with ideas, they get to see them printed in a booklet, they get a blurb on TV, and they get a pat on the back by the president. If people in the private sector figure out a way to increase productivity, they get more money! Who has the most incentive to figure out a way of actually increasing productivity?

5. More government programs: The 1992 riots in Los Angeles shocked the nation. To show their concern for the city, the victims, and their relatives, President Bush and the people who want his job all visited "the war zone." All expressed shock and dismay. All were understanding, caring and compassionate. And all had the same response—more government programs.

Bush said that Congress should send emergency aid, and it did—$1.9 billion in another urban aid program. Clinton said that wasn't enough and that he would do more if elected president.

Only one senior politician, Jack Kemp, Secretary of Housing and Urban Development (HUD), talked about innovative strategies. He noted that we have spent over $2 trillion since we started the Great Society's "War on Poverty" in 1965, and only have more poverty to show for it. He argued in favor of letting those who live in government-owned housing take over ownership of that housing. His argument was simple. People have an incentive to take care of what they own, not burn it down. The point is not that Jack Kemp is a genius, but that serious discussion about tossing out the failed policies of the past is rare.

Repairing the Los Angeles damage is just a part of the push by Clinton to say that his administration would "rebuild America" by having the government spend more money on roads, high–tech telecommunications, and environmental technology. This is nothing new; it is more government spending with new buzzwords like infrastructure used as justification.

Unless the incentives of politicians are changed, they will continue to throw good money down rat holes because it does not cost them anything. Political leaders are not like business leaders. Ford lost a pile of money on the Edsel and Coca–Cola lost a bunch on New Coke; they took their lumps and got on with business. If taxpayers were forced to bail them out we might all be driving Edsels and drinking New Coke.

We Reap What We Sow

The old policy platitudes about how to get the country going are heard over and over from politicians, each claiming to be the one who will do things differently. But we hear the same old song, with 1992 lyrics, from Bush and Clinton. They do not want to discuss the basic truth about government programs, which is that everybody responds to changing incentives. **To understand whether a government program can help or harm our prospects for higher economic growth means we must look at how a program changes the incentive structure.**

Every change in tax rates has an incentive effect on individuals and businesses. That is the most simple proposition ever discovered by economists, philosophers, moralists, sociologists, and psychologists alike. **Throwing taxpayers' money at economic and social problems rarely has any positive long-term effect because it does not improve the incentive structure.**

Many government programs give people incentives not to move in a direction that would help them and the nation. Consider what we do in the Aid to Families with Dependent Children (AFDC) program. Any attempt to save money destroys a family's eligibility for AFDC help. Thus, saving to help a child go to college is discouraged. Saving to make a down payment on a small house is discouraged too. And a recipient who gets even a part–time job will see benefits cut dollar for dollar; work is punished. Getting married and living with the father of your children is punished.

An examination of the regulations that go along with government welfare programs shows the same result: The incentives are negative for individuals to do anything positive about their future. Facing budget difficulties, some state governments have recognized the problem and are attempting to give those on welfare incentives to work and improve their lives. The federal government has done nothing.

When predicting what people will do, it is safest to assume that they will figure out what is best for them—what they want the most—which is not necessarily what is best for the nation. **People respond to incentives no matter what their race, religion, cultural upbringing, income, or education.**

The Incentives Facing Politicians

Politicians are people, too. Therefore, their behavior can be analyzed and predicted. How can politicians at the federal level get reelected election after election after election? They have to be able to raise large sums of money for each election. These campaign funds and assistance can only be obtained if the politicians have something to give out once they are elected and reelected. They can also make voters happy by giving out piles of goodies so they will troop to the polls to send them back to deliver more goodies.

Now consider a world with small government, low taxes, low government spending, little regulation. What do politicians who want to get reelected have to offer those who agree to line election campaign coffers with millions of dollars? Not much. In contrast, consider politicians seeking reelection help today. The federal government controls over 25 percent of our National Income. And politicians oversee thousands of regulations that can make life easier or harder. The federal tax code, in spite of supposed simplification in 1986, is the most complicated it has ever been. **Politicians seeking reelection can offer a**

**lot to potential contributors to reelection campaign
funds.**

Politicians can promise—and deliver—spending programs in contributors' home towns. Politicians can promise
an industry looking for a special tax break the possibility of
that break. Politicians in the world of big government can
offer so much more than can politicians in the world of few
taxes, low government spending, and minimal government
regulation. **The ability to get reelected for life inherently
leads politicians to want the federal government to
increase in size and power.**

Higher Growth Rates in the Future?

Today we have a federal tax system that continues to
become increasingly complicated and is on the verge of
slapping higher and higher penalties on "the rich." We have
the largest federal government deficits we have ever had in
peace time. We have a federal government that spends over
a quarter of National Income, regulates much of the rest,
and state and local governments that spend another 15%.

The combined effect of these burdens mean that there is
little hope for even modest economic growth rates in the
future. In the past, periods of low growth and recession
have been met with cries for expansionary government
fiscal and monetary policy. Whatever positive effect such
policies may have had, they won't work today or in the
future as we will discuss in the next chapter. Macro-
economic planning will not change the problems facing the
macro economy. Our economic problems really stem from
the incentives faced by *individual* citizens as workers and
savers. Their incentives, and those of businesses as produ-
cers and investors are increasingly perverse. Given the
political reality of the incentives facing politicians who
wish to get reelected, we can not expect such negative

incentives to be improved.

Our government is having us eat tomorrow's income. Our national debt of more than $4 trillion and our Social Security debt of more than $12 trillion tell us the truth. **Generations that follow us will see no improvement in their standard of living unless there is substantial economic growth. But with the current political structure, there is little hope that substantial economic growth can ever occur.**

Chapter 9

Prime the Pump?

Every time there is a downturn in the economy, we wait with bated breath for the latest pronouncement from the president and other politicians. Reporters ask them what are *they* going to do to get the economy growing? After all, they run for office claiming they know what needs to be done. Every presidential candidate asserts that he is a wizard who can prime the pump that will fuel economic prosperity.

The belief that the president and Congress can make the economy grow dates back to sometime during the Great Depression. President Franklin Roosevelt was told by his advisors that he and the Congress could "get America moving again" with the policies of the New Deal. This idea next appeared in the Employment Act of 1946, which charged the federal government with the responsibility of promoting high employment. This notion hit the high point with the Full Employment and Balanced Growth Act of 1978, in which Congress committed the government to full employment, which was defined as 4% unemployment. (Obviously, none of these laws worked as advertised.)

There is a way for the president and especially

Congress to get the American economy growing. They have to give up much of what they control. But that control is exactly how members of Congress guarantee themselves lifetime jobs. The more resources they control and the more regulations they generate, the more they reap in reelection campaign help from those seeking government goodies, regulatory relief, and special tax treatment. Because Congress has no incentive to give up control over the things that are stifling the economy, we are treated to the traditional policy prescriptions for growth. Let's look at the usual suspects—monetary and fiscal policy.

Pump Money into the Economy

The Federal Reserve System (the Fed) is our central bank. It controls the quantity of money in circulation by buying and selling U.S. government Treasury bonds. There are a lot of bonds to buy and sell since we have a $4 trillion national debt financed by Treasury bonds. When the Fed buys Treasury bonds it hands over new money it has created, which goes into circulation. When it sells bonds, it takes in cash, thereby taking money out of circulation.

The Fed can also affect the amount of money in circulation by changing the discount rate—the interest rate at which it will lend banks money—or the reserve requirements for all depository institutions—that is, how much money banks must keep "in the vault." So the Fed can pump money into the economy or take it out.

An "easy money" or "easy credit" policy, which occurs when the Fed pumps more money into the economy (increases the money supply), can have an initial positive effect on the general economy. But easy money and credit only have positive effects in the short run, and sometimes not at all if enough people understand what is going on. Just look at what happened to the U.S. economy under the easy money of the 70s and early 80s.

The money supply increased an average of 10% per year from 1971 to 1983. The result was inflation and high interest rates. Home mortgage rates had averaged 6% in the 60s, but they rose steadily through the 70s, hitting a high of over 15% in 1982. The Consumer Price Index (the rate of inflation) rose 13% a year in 1979 and in 1980. The result of this easy money policy, as we all know, was no real economic growth during that time period. We are still paying the cost of these foolish policies, because the wild swings in interest rates and the recession of the early 80s that wrung the inflation out of the economy were major causes of the bankruptcy of so many savings and loans.

When the Fed starts priming the pump with high money growth, the only thing that can happen eventually is inflation and more inflation. Workers get wise and demand cost-of-living clauses in their contract. Sellers of raw materials won't sign long-term contracts without escalator clauses that let them raise prices as inflation goes up. Those who lease buildings put in escalator clauses too.

Having learned a very costly lesson from these earlier easy money policies, many people now watch money supply figures very closely. They make predictions about what will happen to interest rates and to the rate of inflation depending on what the Fed does. It is virtually impossible to fool anybody anymore with easy money.

If the Fed increases the money growth rate now, people respond right away by raising interest rates in anticipation of higher future rates of inflation. High interest rates hurt development and economic growth in the long run. They also add to the amount of interest that has to be paid on the national debt because the federal government, like everyone else, must borrow money at the going interest rate.

The game of easy credit used to be a way to prime the pump in the short run. It never worked in the long run because, even without all the Fed watchers, people eventually learned. **Now that money supply numbers are watched daily, the probability that the Fed can fool the public is virtually zero. So much for easy credit as a way to increase economic growth.**

Keynesian Deficit Spending

If you took a class in economics anytime after World War II, you found the standard treatment of fiscal policy, which is defined in most textbooks as changes in government spending and taxes to affect employment and economic growth. The policy prescription is simple: If the economy is overheated, reduce government spending or increase taxes to cool it down. It is hard to understand what an overheated economy is; we certainly have not had too high of a rate of growth in memory, so it must refer to when there is high inflation.

On the other hand, if the economy is not growing and there is too much unemployment, the policy prescription is to increase government spending or reduce taxes to get it moving. This latter policy has been called Keynesian deficit spending, based on the famous 1936 book by John Maynard Keynes called *The General Theory*.

The problem with using deficit government spending to get the economy moving is that the extra spending is financed by borrowing, which normally reduces private investment. This is the so-called crowding-out effect which works as follows: The government issues Treasury bonds to finance the deficit. If the Fed buys those bonds from the Treasury, it must "print" money to give to the Treasury (the government) to spend, increasing the supply of money, and, thereby, inflation.

Alternatively, the Treasury offers its bonds to private investors. As the government competes to borrow money, interest rates will rise. As interest rates rise, private borrowing for investment gets crowded out to make way for government deficit spending. No new long–term economic growth is created. There is simply an increase in spending by the public sector offset by a decrease in spending by the private sector.

Even if the crowding out of private investment did not occur, deficit spending makes little sense to think about as a cure for our economic woes. We have had federal budget deficits constantly for over 20 years and now have the largest deficit in history. **If a $400 billion federal deficit isn't enough to get the economy moving, then what is?**

The simple fact that deficit spending will not spur real economic growth was apparently lost on hundreds of economists who signed a statement in 1992 calling on the federal government to increase the deficit even more! Their argument was Keynesian with no apology. Yes, they said, there was a large deficit. But getting the economy out of the recession was more important than worrying about the size of the deficit. So the government should spend more.

This a remarkable line of reasoning. The federal government is already spending a larger percentage of our national income than during any peacetime period in history. Over 40% of National Income is already spent by government. Is that not high enough? Strangely, these economists do not call for the other Keynesian policy prescription—tax cuts. The tax cuts of the Kennedy and Reagan administrations both led to good periods of economic growth and increased employment. But economists who favor big government are blind to the obvious success of that simple policy.

Finally, there is no statistical evidence that links increased federal government deficits with positive changes in national output and employment. **Twenty years of federal deficits have produced near zero real growth in the private sector.** Any policy prescriptions that involve new government programs to prime the pump via deficit spending are simply smokescreens for the real desire of politicians and their friends who support such programs. That desire is to increase their power over resources in order to get reelected again.

Can We Grow?

Knowing that George Bush, Bill Clinton, or any other human cannot use magical fiscal or monetary policies to get us growing, what can we say about growth? What we know about growth is both simple and complicated. What is simple is that we know that growth occurs when there are incentives to save and invest. What is complicated is how the growth mechanism works. Economic growth does not happen by having the nation's corporate leaders or politicians sit around and decide where investment should occur. It is by the competitive process of trial and error that entrepreneurs find where investment has the highest rate of return.

Americans currently are discouraged from saving and investing, which means our growth rate is lower than it could be. Let's see how we treat savers. Suppose a couple looking toward retirement invested $10,000 in 1971 in the stock market. Twenty years later they sold the stock for $35,000. A nice gain? No, adjusted for inflation, the $10,000 invested in 1971 is the same as $34,000 in 1991. Their actual gain is $1,000. An additional problem is that taxes must be paid on the $25,000 "gain" the government claims was made. Because most people pay state income taxes as well as federal income taxes, taxes would be about $8,000. The $27,000 left from the $35,000 is worth 20% less than the money originally invested. These investors were punished for saving funds to help cover their retirement years.

German investors would have paid no tax on a gain from a long–term investment. Some countries, like England, tax gains, but only after they have been adjusted for inflation. In this case, there would have been a tax on $1,000, since that was the only real gain. **Among developed nations we have one of the highest tax rates on capital gains, the earnings on savings that are invested. And we wonder why Americans are not thrifty like the Germans and Japanese?**

The U.S. has double taxation on the earnings from savings invested in shares of corporations. Suppose you have $10,000 invested in IBM stock. IBM must pay 33% federal income tax on its earnings after it pays all operating expenses. After it has paid federal taxes (and some state taxes too), the earnings left are shared by the stockholders —who then pay income taxes on their earnings. These earnings can come from IBM in dividends or in the increased stock price when they sell the stock for a higher price than they bought it for. This double whammy means the expected rate of return must be pretty high for investment to occur. Remember, a saver faces the risk of losing the funds invested if the stock price falls (and there is no tax deduction allowed for such losses). If there is a gain, it must be greater than inflation to mean anything, but even the gain that is wiped out by inflation is hit by the double taxation on all gains.

High taxes on investment and the inability to write off investment losses against income gains discourage saving. They also reduce investment in risky ventures that may produce exciting inventions. It is much safer for savers to stick with the tried and true—like government bonds that keep the national debt afloat. Further, as we discussed before, the current large federal deficit means the government is borrowing as much money as people are saving, making fewer funds available for private investment.

To break economic gridlock we must change government policies that discourage saving and investment. Only by increased saving and investment will we raise our economic growth rate, push wages up, increase tax revenues, and reduce poverty.

No Investment, No Growth

Growth can only occur if we sacrifice today. The equation is simple: growth requires investment, which comes from saving. The larger the percentage of total income that goes to saving, the greater the potential for investment and, hence, growth.

We have two big problems; personal saving rates have fallen and government deficits have gone up. Back in 1970 people saved 7% of personal income. The deficit was equal to 22% of the saving, leaving the other 78% for investment in the private sector. By 1991, people saved 4.5% of their income, a decline of 36% in the personal saving rate, and the deficit was equal to 90% of the saving, leaving only 10% for private investment.

There have been many explanations for why the rate of saving and investment is so dismal in the U.S. We are told that we just aren't as thrifty as the Japanese and the Germans. We are told that we are too impatient and want too much today. We are told that we have lived a soft life too long. We are told lots of things, most of them at best half truths and others completely beside the point.

The main reason for the low rate of saving and investment is that the federal government commandeers a larger and larger share of saving each year because of huge budget deficits. Foreigners help out by buying some of the debt, but most is purchased by Americans—individuals, pension plans, corporate money managers, and so on.

But the Government Could Invest

Financing the federal budget deficit bleeds saving out of the private sector where it would be used for investment that would get our growth rate back on track. But, some say, the government can invest too. That is correct. If the deficit were generated by the federal government investing in assets that would add to the nation's future productive capacity, then budget deficits would have little negative effect on our growth rate. In fact, such deficits could even increase our growth rate if they created more investment than would have occurred had the funds stayed in the private sector and only been used for current consumption.

The same argument applies to taxes. If the government taxed us to add to future productive capacity, then our growth rate could be made greater than it would be otherwise. What the federal government does with its tax revenues and its deficit financing is exactly the opposite. Most of the federal budget goes to entitlements—subsidies to farmers, welfare payments, Social Security, medicare payments, and so on.

The Government Accounting Office reports that government spending on what might be called investment has been falling. Spending on the nation's highways, mass transit, water and sewer systems, and other public facilities took about 4% of GDP in the late 1960s. By the late 1980s that had fallen to about 2% of GDP. **The explosion of government spending on entitlements has not only increased our taxes, increased the deficit, consumed the savings from lower defense spending, but it has been eating into the physical facilities of the country.**

While the government is involved in spending categories that represent investment activities—research, education, and highways for example—even this spending is filled with waste. Most government projects are inefficient and have little connection to what has the highest rate of return to society. What we call federal investments include boondoggles that have almost no value; the money is mostly wasted. So even when the government conducts so-called investment spending, the results are no better than the results in the former USSR where the central planners decided what investment would take place.

The long and the short of this argument is clear: **Only by investment in the private sector, not by more spending on government consumption, can the economy have sustained growth over time.** The old policy prescriptions of easy credit and deficit financing will not work. Only cutting the barriers to growth by providing more incentives for private investment can have any lasting effect on the rate of economic growth in this country or in any other.

Are Americans Dumb Couch Potatoes?

Some would argue that America cannot grow even if such barriers to growth are removed and more incentives for investment are provided. They contend that Americans are not as smart and do not work as hard as the Japanese or the Germans. Indeed, the Japanese seem to believe that Americans are lazy. Such claims are completely beside the point and are probably false.

For example, Germans enjoy more vacation days than almost anybody and certainly more than the average American. The average German worker gets six weeks paid vacation per year, plus fifteen paid legal holidays. Most Americans still only get two to four weeks vacation, plus another eight to ten paid legal holidays. Germans work hundreds of hours a year less than Americans, but are more productive and have rising wages because there is constant investment in new productive capital.

So it is not lack of work by American workers that can explain why our rate of economic growth is so low. It is, rather, our policies that provide incentives not to save and not to invest. The Japanese and the Germans have explicit high–growth incentives to encourage saving and investment. Imagine the amount of investment and capital in the United States if we had a tax policy similar to that in Hong Kong, Japan, or Germany. The rate of saving and investment would skyrocket compared to what it is today. We would have high economic growth as Japan, Hong Kong, and Germany have had for so many years.

Occasionally, the president comes up with a rehashed idea to help increase investment. President Bush proposes an investment tax credit, so that some investment income would be taxed at a lower rate than income not invested. But we have had that one before. The problem with such a credit is that no one knows how long it will last. **It is hard for business to plan rationally when the government keeps changing the rules time and again. Incentives mean everything. If the economy is to move again and have a strong economic growth rate, the incentive structure has to be changed to encourage more work, more saving, and more investing.**

Policy Makers Know the Truth

Members of Congress are not ignorant of what we have just said. Most are very intelligent people who know how to get reelected to high office time and again. Almost any member of Congress could tell you, in private, much of what is written in this book, or could be convinced of the intellectual validity of what is in this book. Does that mean that members of Congress, so informed, will go out and ask for a reduction in federal spending and taxes and a change in the incentive structure facing savers and investors? The answer is clearly no.

Politicians often know what is right, but no *one* politician can make any change. They get reelected for "bringing home the bacon." Bringing home the bacon requires a pig to be slaughtered. The pig is the private income we all generate. When it is carved up, the larger the share of the pig that can be captured by Congress, the more bacon each politician can take home and divvy up among those who support the reelection of that member of Congress. **We cannot hope for members of Congress to reduce the size of the slice of bacon they take to the folks back home, unless they have fewer incentives to do so.**

Chapter 10

Who Pays What?

When economic times are good and the economy is growing, wages rise. People can look forward to a better standard of living by working hard. But when an economy is stagnant and wages are steady, a way to a better standard of living is to take what someone else has.

At the crudest level, people steal from other people. When unemployment rises, that is, when people have a hard time earning a living, there is more theft and burglary. At a more polite and legal level, when economies are stagnant, people become more interested in hearing from politicians about the wealth someone else has that could make their lives better. **Economic growth is beneficial not only because it makes people happier materially, but because it reduces political tension.**

In the early 1990s, while the economy has been stagnant, there has been more talk about the rich not paying their "fair share" of taxes, and tax rates on higher incomes have been on the rise. The persistent high deficit, which most voters do not like, gives added reason to favor tax increases. "Let us raise taxes on the rich and the budget will be balanced," say some politicians. Few politicians are foolish enough to advocate general tax hikes. But if the taxes are to be paid by "the rich," maybe it's not such a bad idea.

What are the popular perceptions about tax burdens? Most polls indicate that people think their tax burdens are a little too high, have been rising, and are likely to go up. They think that waste in government is a major problem and is worst at the federal level. Similarly, taxpayers think they get the most value for their tax dollar at the local level and that local taxes are the most fair. Most people think a tax cut would stimulate the economy, but that politicians talk about tax–cut gimmicks, not substantive tax reform.

The Tax Tale

Economists are not very good at figuring out who pays taxes. We know that the Social Security tax, which is "shared" by employers and employees, is mostly paid by the employee. An employer knows that the tax is a cost of hiring a worker, so it is figured into the wage bill. Less clear are taxes on businesses. Do businesses absorb taxes by reducing profits, or do they pass the taxes on to consumers? Studies indicate that it seems to be a mix. In any event, citizens own businesses and property, so one way or another we all pay the taxes.

Taxes cause changes in incentives, so they have consequences beyond their immediate cost. But for now we will just concern ourselves with some measures of the general tax burden—what the average worker and household pays one way or another. Governments collected over $6,000 in taxes for every person in the country in 1990. Per person, local governments collected $800, state governments $1,250, and the federal government $4,000.

The Tax Foundation reports "Tax Freedom Day" for the average American. Looking at a year's income, how long into the year did the average worker have to work just to pay federal, state, and local taxes for the year? In 1992, workers finished paying taxes on May 5. The day keeps getting later in the year. In 1990 it was May 3, in 1980 it was May 1, in 1970 it was April 26, in 1960 it was April 16, in 1950 it was April 3, and in 1940 it was March 8.

Another way to think of taxes is to look at what share of income earned by the average worker in an 8 hour work day goes to taxes. In 1992, 2 hours and 45 minutes are spent working to pay taxes. That is about the same amount of time spent working to pay for housing, clothing, and food. Of that time, 59 minutes are for state and local taxes; one hour and 46 minutes are for federal taxes.

Here is a "typical" family budget for a married couple, both working, with two children. Their total income in 1991 was $53,265. That amount made them the median family— right in the middle of the nation's two–worker families. Of that, over $20,000 went to various taxes, leaving them $33,000 for everything else. Of their income that went to taxes, a quarter went to state and local taxes and three-quarters went to federal taxes. **The amount of taxes paid by the average family was more than the family spent on housing, food, and health care combined.**

AVERAGE FAMILY BUDGET, 1991

Category	Amount	Percent
Taxes	$ 20,187	37.9
Housing	8,895	16.7
Food	6,072	11.4
Health Care	4,847	9.1
Transportation	3,995	7.5
Recreation	2,557	4.8
Clothing	2,397	4.5
Everything Else	4,315	8.1
Total	**$ 53,265**	**100.0**

Most politicians would call this family "upper–middle class." What has happened to this median family's income? Inflation adjusted, family after–tax income in 1991 is right where it was in 1986. **Real incomes have gone up since 1986, but taxes have gone up faster, stripping away the gains for the "average" American.**

Federal tax rates are the same across the country, but state and local taxes vary quite a bit. The state that taxed the least in 1992 was South Dakota, which took 44 minutes of income from an 8–hour work day. At the high end of state taxes was New York, which took 79 minutes from an 8 hour work day. With the highest tax rates in the land, Governor Cuomo of New York marched in Washington in May of 1992 to demand *more* federal money for New York. The South Dakota governor was at home.

Some wealthy people such as former President Carter are paid large speaking fees to express concern that "the rich" are not paying their "fair share" of federal taxes. Let's look at the federal income tax bill paid by different income groups.

FEDERAL INCOME TAXES PAID BY GROUP

Income Group	1980	1990	Change (%)
Highest 1%	18.2%	25.4%	+40
Highest 5%	36.0	44.1	+23
Highest 10%	48.8	56.1	+15
Highest 20%	66.0	71.8	+ 9
Lowest 60%	13.8	11.0	−20
Lowest 40%	3.6	2.4	−33
Lowest 20%	−0.2	−0.5	−150

Given recent changes in the tax law, which stripped away deductions for higher income taxpayers, the top 5% income earners now pay about 50% of the federal tax bill. **The top 1% income earners now pay about 30% of the federal tax bill.** What a "fair share" of the federal tax bill is for any income group is a matter of opinion, but it is clear that high income earners are picking up a larger and larger share of the federal tax bill.

The Reagan tax revisions of 1981 and 1986 made the federal tax system more "progressive" than it was during the Carter years—the rich pay a greater share of their income in taxes and pay a greater share of the income tax bill now than they did before. Nevertheless, the claim is made that "the rich" should pay more. Politicians know this line is easy to sell. Most of us would be happy to have someone else pay for more federal goodies.

As a practical matter, what can we squeeze out of the rich? There are about 65,000 taxpayers with incomes over $1 million. Let's consider the common proposal to increase their federal tax rate by 25%. That would add less than $7 billion in tax revenues. That does not put much of a dent in a $400 billion deficit, and adds less than one-half of one percent to the $1.5 trillion budget. Members of Congress understand what a drop in the bucket this is, so they are not talking about higher taxes for millionaires, but higher taxes for several million people making around $100,000 a year—the top 5% of income earners.

Higher tax rates for high-income earners are already in place, which may have something to do with why the economy has been so sluggish. Working to earn higher income is being punished with higher taxes. In 1992, the top federal rate increased from 28% to 31%—an 11% increase. Besides the tax rate increase, there are fewer deductions. For married couples with incomes over $100,000, deductions such as mortgage interest, charitable

contributions, and state and local taxes are all being
stripped away. And for married couples with incomes over
$150,000 and single individuals with incomes over
$100,000, the personal exemptions are stripped away.

Does Fairness Matter?

The problem with taxing "the rich" is not a matter of
fairness. There is no way to determine what is tax fairness.
Some people will argue that everyone should pay the same
proportion of their income; others will argue that as
incomes rise, one should pay a higher proportion of his or
her income; and there are other views. In any event,
fairness is certainly not the basis for how tax policy is
determined in the real world.

**The biggest problem with taxing "the rich" is that
they are a major source of saving—and investment—in
the economy.** If that saving is taxed away, the money will
be spent by the government and will not be available to
finance new economic development.

Former California Governor Jerry Brown, when running
for the Democratic nomination for president in 1992, talked
about a flat income tax. Except for a few deductions, all
income would be taxed at the same 13% rate. The press
treated this notion as if Brown had lost his marbles. But his
point was simple: A low flat tax would raise as much
revenue as our progressive tax scheme and, more importantly, would stimulate economic activity.

The present tax system, which encourages special
interests to lobby for (and get) special tax treatment, causes
great economic waste and distortion. Millions of people
spend billions of hours each year fiddling with their tax
returns. That time is pure economic waste—no one is
creating anything doing taxes and, we presume, no one is
having fun doing it. We also hire numerous lawyers and

accountants to help do our taxes—more wasteful activity by talented people.

Besides the cost of dealing with the tax system, we must add the economic distortions caused by differential tax rates. People spend countless hours and many dollars rearranging their activities to reduce tax burdens. This causes over–investment in some activities and under–investment in other activities. **The loss to our economy caused by having something other than a simple flat tax is estimated to run easily into the hundreds of billions of dollars each year.**

Those who claim that our convoluted "progressive" tax system is "fair," and that it would be made "more fair" by being even "more progressive," must explain what is fair about destroying economic activity that would benefit all members of society. **Politicians will never adopt an economically rational tax system as long as their careers are enhanced by helping to get tax breaks for special interests and as long as they can tell people that they are making someone else pay the bill for their government.**

Chapter 11

Preying on the Poor

Americans have a tradition of sympathy for the poor. This is not a universal feeling around the world. In many countries the poor are viewed with disgust; there is no milk of human kindness, and little help is provided. But most Americans come from poor families because we are a nation of immigrants. Most Americans can tell stories of ancestors who endured poverty for the sake of a better world for their children. Americans want the underdog to succeed.

Many politicians tell us we should feel guilty about poverty. We are told that the tens of billions of dollars we give in private charity and pay in taxes to support numerous poverty programs are not enough. **Politicians tell us that poverty can be cured only by more taxes and more government programs. If you do not agree, you are called insensitive and greedy.**

It is not polite for politicians to tell people they want to be elected so they will have the power to take money from one person to give it to another person (in exchange for campaign support and votes). To talk about taking from one rich person to help 99 poor people sounds much more polite, even Christian to some, and may win a lot of votes.

It is not called taking from the rich; it is called making them pay their "fair share."

Most people are sympathetic toward the poor and want to help them and their children have a decent life. Most people believe that the government should help the poor and are willing to pay taxes to help the truly deserving. The problem is not a lack of will to help the poor. **The problem is that our political leaders have wasted hundreds of billions of our dollars creating a permanent underclass that has little reason or ability to abandon poverty.**

We have a poverty industry. It is directed by politicians, fed by tax dollars, supports a massive bureaucracy, and does little to help the truly deserving. Let us examine who we are supposed to be helping and how much has been done in the name of helping the poor. We spend hundreds of billions of dollars each year in the name of helping the poor. How come there are still so many poor people?

Counting the Poor

Poverty is not naturally related to race, sex, color, creed, or national origin. It is a function of different backgrounds, opportunities, barriers, and the incentives people face. What do we find in America? When incomes are adjusted for inflation, the same percentage of households have incomes under $10,000 per year now as was the case before the "War on Poverty" started in the late 1960s. Inflation adjusted, **in 1968, 17% of all households had income under $10,000; in 1988, 17% of all households had income under $10,000. For black households, the situation has worsened a little. In 1968, 31% had inflation adjusted incomes under $10,000; in 1988, 34% had incomes under $10,000.** $10,000 a year income is an arbitrary definition of poverty, but let's use it as a yardstick to see where the problem appears to be worst and what is being done about it.

In 1990, there were over 94 million households in the U.S. These included households with children headed by one or two adults, households headed by two adults with no children, and single adult households. Of these households, 23.5% reported money income under $10,000. **If we take into account the taxes they paid, the tax credits they received, the cash received from various government programs, and the value of non-cash benefits such as food stamp and medical assistance, the number of households with income under $10,000 falls in half.**

Another government study shows that the poorest 20% of all households earned a money income of about $7,500 in 1990. But, taking into account the various public benefits received, their income rose to $15,000. That is, the average household in the bottom 20% of the income distribution doubled its income from taxpayer–provided benefits.

Most benefits go to those who have almost no income; that is, people who never or rarely work. In 1990, 16.4% of the population had money incomes under $5,000 a year, but after various benefits were received, only 2.8% of the population had incomes under $5,000 a year. Obviously the poor are not made rich by welfare, but help is provided. Where does the money for this help come from? The upper–income earners provide most of it. In 1990, 4.5% of all households started with money income over $100,000, but after taxes only 2.2% of all households had income over $100,000.

Do the Rich Get Richer?

Some people are born to wealth. Unless they fritter it all away, they are called rich. Some people spend their lives in poverty; they are called poor. The poor are always with us, but **who is poor and who is rich changes.** Census Bureau data divide families into fifths, or quintiles. The data show that each year 18% of the families in the lowest quintile move up into a higher income bracket. Of the people in the highest quintile, about 22% fall into a lower income bracket each year. That is, for most people there is substantial income mobility—one of the great benefits of a market economy.

A recent study by the Treasury Department tells an interesting story about the rich and the poor. The study followed Americans from 1979 to 1988. The richest 1% income earners in 1979 were still doing well in 1988, but less than half were still in the top 1%. In fact, 2.2% of the people who were among the 1% richest in 1979 had fallen to the poorest income group (the lowest 20%) by 1988. **Most of the rich do not just get richer.**

What about the poor? The Treasury study found that of those in the bottom fifth in 1979, only 14.2% were still in the bottom 20% in 1988. That is, only one person in seven was still in the poorest income group nine years later. Of those who were in the bottom fifth in 1979, 14.7% had moved into the top income group by 1988. That is, more people had risen to the top income group in nine years than had remained in the bottom income group. Furthermore, over half of those in the bottom fifth in 1979 had reached the top half of all income earners in 1988. **Most of the poor do not just get poorer.**

Another study by the Urban Institute followed the richest people and the poorest people from 1977 to 1986. The income of the one–fifth of all families with the highest income in 1977 increased an average of 5% by 1986. The income of the one-fifth of all families with the lowest income in 1977 increased an average of 77% by 1986. As the authors said, **"the rich got a little richer and the poor got much richer."**

How Poor Is Poor?

Why do incomes rise and fall? Some of the fluctuation is due to economic fortune or misfortune. Some of it is due to hard work; some is due to laziness. But most of it is due to the natural life–cycle of earnings. Many young adults have low income and, therefore, are counted as poor. **Many medical and law students have low income and are counted as poor.** We have no reason to worry about such people—they are on the road to high earnings. We would not think of them as the "deserving poor."

Many retired people have low income and so are defined as poor. But many have higher–than–average wealth because they own their home and other assets. They are called poor by the government because their income is low. We would not call most of these people the "deserving poor."

Consider what Census Bureau data reveal about those who are counted as poor. **Of the 30 million people defined as living in poverty because of their low income, 38% own their own homes, 1/2 million own homes worth more than $100,000, 62% own a car, and 14% own two or more cars.** These households spent $1.94 for every $1 of reported income, because they receive various public benefits and because many are in the "cash economy," earning income not reported to the government.

Despite the fact that some people counted as poor are not really poor, there are people trapped in poverty; nearly everyone would agree that they are the deserving poor. **When a politician says that millions of families have incomes less than $10,000 a year, they are not telling us much; many of these people are not the deserving poor.** A $10,000 a year income is low, but it does not tell us if there is a problem we should be worried about. We may be talking about law students, retired folks who are pretty

comfortable, or other people most of us would not call
really needy.

Where Is Poverty Worst?

The best cure for poverty is a job. That seems so simple
as to be silly, but it is one of life's truths. Of course there
are some people in this group we would call the "working
poor," but most American poverty is not related to wages
being too low, but to people who will not or cannot work.

We saw before that, in 1990, 23.5% of all households
reported money income under $10,000 a year. But only
2.8% of households with one full–time employed worker
had income under $10,000. Similarly, 16.4% of all house-
holds reported income under $5,000 a year, but less than
one percent of all households with one full–time employed
worker have incomes under $5,000. **Unemployment or
other misfortune can cause poverty, but this situation is
temporary for most people. Adults who can and will
work are not threatened by the prospect of a lifetime in
grinding poverty.**

A government study looked at income in 1989 as a
function of family situation. The study reports who makes
above and below the median (mid–point) income in the
U.S. That is, half the population had income less than the
median; half the population had income above the median.
In this study, the poor are defined as those whose income
was only one–quarter of the median income of the entire
population. In 1989, 8.3% of the population had income
less than one–quarter of the median income in the country.

Who was *least* likely to be poor; that is, to earn less than
one–quarter of the median income? The answer is: adults in
married families with husband and wife present; only 3.2%
of such people were in the poor category. Who was *most*
likely to earn less than one–quarter of the median income?

Women with children but no spouse; 47% of all women with children under age 6 who did not have a spouse at home were in the lowest income category. Because there were 3.4 million women with over 4 million children in 1989 in that situation, this is a major social problem.

TV's Murphy Brown aside, if you are a single woman with a child, you are likely to be poor, regardless of race. Over 42% of all white women and 53% of all black women with children under age 6 and no spouse present earn less than one–quarter of the median income. The situation improves a little bit when the children are older and off to school, but the poverty rate among this group is still very high.

This poverty is particularly noticeable among blacks, because 40% of all black women aged 18 to 65 have children under 18 and have no spouse at home. This compares to 20% of Hispanic women and 10% of white women who are in similar situations. This problem is getting worse. The number of women (and children) in such households has tripled in the last 25 years. **The facts are clear; if a woman has children but no spouse, she and the children are very likely to be in poverty.**

In contrast, family stability means low poverty rates regardless of race. For example, among married black women between 20 and 44 who work full–time, only 0.8% earned less than one–quarter of the median income. Indeed, 66% of these women earned *more* than the national median income; and 73% of married black women between 45 and 64 who worked full time earned more than the median income.

Wringing Our Hands

The Los Angeles riots in May 1992 renewed concern about the poor. A typical reaction was this statement from a magazine: "...what we have just witnessed in Los Angeles is a glimpse of a racial and urban crisis in this country that is steadily growing in intensity. Neither Republican neglect nor traditional Democratic liberalism comes close to solving it. It's time to start over." That is, the Reagan and Bush administrations have not spent enough, and the billions spent in liberal welfare programs have not solved the poverty problem, so we need more and different taxpayer–supported programs.

The poverty problem has become a social sickness. We now have generations of families raised on the welfare system. They do not live well; they are in poverty; but it is what they know. They know that their standard of living goes up if they have children. **The government pays teenage girls to have children. By having children, unmarried teenage girls become welfare adults—eligible for their own monthly welfare, their own apartment, payments for the children, and other benefits.**

Everyone who looks at this system agrees that it is sick. It encourages irresponsible behavior and people who are perfectly capable of working are punished if they try to leave welfare. **Most single women with children would suffer a drop in income if they took a job. To trap people in welfare and, worse yet, have them raise their children in a welfare system, is economically destructive and, by any standard, morally bankrupt as it forces the destruction of families.**

But welfare reform is scary to those who rely on welfare—it is all they know. Politicians who want their votes cannot risk losing those voters by threatening to take away what they know. The incentives of our elected leaders lead them to do the wrong thing. They dribble out a little support to a lot of people to maximize the number of votes they get in return. **Politicians are preying on the poor and on our sympathies for the poor.** The result is a travesty.

Instead of giving good nutritious meals to the truly needy, food stamps are passed out to over 25 million people, most of whom are in no danger of malnutrition. Instead of giving generous public assistance to the truly deserving, Congress has declared that many able–bodied adults are due an entitlement to a support that destroys their incentive to work their way out of poverty. **Our political leaders know the welfare system is sick. They will not reform it because they are returned to Congress again and again even though they are responsible for this horrible system.**

Chapter 12

Resegregating America

The Los Angeles riots in 1992 were not just a protest over the failure to convict the police who beat Rodney King; they were a sign of the social sickness and criminals that are endemic in low income minority communities. The Los Angeles Watts riots of 1965 could be attributed to the frustrations faced by blacks who had been denied equal opportunity and long condemned to the bottom of the economic barrel. **The 1992 riots occurred after hundreds of billions of dollars had been spent in the name of help for the black community.**

The rioters and, of more concern, the non–rioters who live in the slums, are the victims of government policies that have denied them the advantages of equal opportunity. They have been made wards of the state with little hope of anything else. Our political leaders are not interested in any change; they just call for more of the destructive policies that have worsened racial tensions in our society. **Our politicians are reelected even though they support policies that produce economic and human tragedy, so they will not change the policies.**

It Will Get Worse

The rapid growth of social programs in the 90s, especially welfare, means that more people will be wards of the state tomorrow than are today. The number of people who take food stamps has increased by a couple of million in the past two years alone. The more we offer people to live on welfare, the more will live on welfare. It happens that blacks are the racial group most affected by these policies. But there are many whites and Hispanics in the same boat.

Because the average income of workers is not rising, but tax burdens are, there will be ever increasing resentment toward those who receive welfare benefits. The cost of supporting those on welfare is rising and the number is too. The Los Angeles rioters were not physically or mentally disabled persons who have been mistreated by society. They were able–bodied people perfectly capable of working. There is little sympathy anywhere for people who take from those who work for a living, seem to spit in their faces, and have the audacity to claim they deserve more. Welfare is supposed to help the truly deserving; everyone can see that is not what is happening. As the cost of supporting the welfare class goes up, resentment will grow.

Success Is Not Due to Race

Achievement does not happen because one belongs to the "right" race. When we look at the income of ethnic groups, we see a reflection of work ethic, educational achievement, and other factors. Among certain groups there is no question that most came to America looking to work hard. Their achievements are not necessarily typical of all people in their country of origin; they have excelled beyond those left in the home country.

Consider the ranking of average household income by

racial group in America, from highest to lowest: Japanese, Indian, Filipino, Cuban, Anglo (whites), Mexicans, Puerto Ricans, Native Americans, and Blacks. The income range from top to bottom is more than two–to–one. That is, the average income of Japanese–American families is more than twice the average of African–American families.

Those at the top got there by working, not because they did not face discrimination or because they received welfare benefits. They never got *trapped* on welfare and they blew past stupid racist attitudes. Fifty years ago the most hated group in the country were Japanese–Americans. They were rounded up and put in prisons during World War II simply because of their race. A generation later, they are at the top of the financial heap.

As could be seen in the Los Angeles riots, the distinction was not minorities versus whites; it was have–nots versus haves. This problem is growing worse because there are more have–nots taking and demanding more. They are resented by the haves who work hard to pay for unappreciated welfare benefits.

Living on Welfare Is the Pits

Living on welfare is dreary—horrible by the standards of those who read this book—but if it is the only life you know, it seems normal. There is little comprehension by many people at the bottom of why things are the way they are; they just know that they don't have much and that they have little chance of getting any more. They are right. The welfare system removes people from normal society where one is expected to go to school and then get a job. While doing well in school and getting a job are rewarded, under our current system, not doing well and not getting a job means more of the same, rather than a worsening of conditions for those on welfare.

What is hard to remember is that most of this terrible situation has arisen in the last 25 years. Back in 1964, when the Civil Rights Act was passed, whites had reason to feel ashamed not only about racist attitudes and actions, but about the legal barriers faced by blacks. In many states, the government provided segregated, miserably funded public schools for black children. Federal and state labor laws, some of which are still on the books, made it hard for blacks to compete in many labor markets. Housing, public transportation, restaurants, motels, stores, and many other parts of life were segregated. Less than 30 years ago, blacks and other racial minorities faced barriers that we have trouble imagining today.

Just when legal segregation began to fall, and blacks obtained the right to a more equal share of funding for education and a chance at employment opportunities previously denied, the "Great Society" came along to shower welfare benefits on the poor. Why this was done is not clear—maybe it was white guilt; or maybe it was an effort to keep many blacks out of the mainstream by trapping them on welfare; but most likely it was simply that politicians like to dump money on the heads of people who can vote. Previously, poor blacks could not vote; now they could.

By 1971, the number of people receiving AFDC, the primary welfare program, had jumped to over 10 million—triple the number of ten years before—despite good economic and employment growth rates in the 1960s. Government policies created a permanent welfare class almost overnight.

Even if the Great Society's welfare programs were intended to help, their effects are perverse. **All of society suffers the cost of supporting a welfare class and the social degeneration that goes with it.**

Don't Rock the Boat

Living on welfare degrades people. It destroys their incentives to care for themselves and their family. Our political leaders know this is true. **Welfare policies will not change because politicians are reelected despite the fact that they keep this sick system in place.**

There are two basic ways to solve the welfare mess, neither of which will fly politically today. One option is to slash welfare benefits except for the physically and mentally disabled. Going cold turkey means hard times for those who would lose benefits and have to learn to work for a living. Those people will punish the politicians who do that to them. The other option is to change the system so we pay people to get off welfare instead of staying on. This would mean increasing the amount we spend on welfare even more, at least for several years, a policy that taxpaying voters do not want to hear about.

Either method will never be accepted in our current political structure, even though the long run results would make everyone better off. No matter how welfare is reformed, the costs would be high for several years, which means members of Congress would get blamed. Some would lose their seats. **Because members of Congress want to stay there for life, they will not risk their seats just for the sake of reform, even though it would help the poor.**

The economics of welfare is just like the economics of farm subsidies. As we saw earlier, the government takes money from taxpayers and gives it to sugar farmers to grow sugar. If we did not give them this money they would do something else more productive. We waste the money taxpayers give farmers in sugar subsidies, and the farmers are wasting their time growing a crop we do not need instead of performing useful work. There are two ways out of this. Cut off the subsidies or buy out the farmers. Just like welfare reform, it is either expensive to the taxpayers or scary to the recipients, so either way Congress is not going to mess with the system.

In this chapter, we could focus on the wasteful farm program, but have chosen welfare because the costs of this program are immense and because the consequences are immoral. The welfare program wastes money on welfare and destroys economic opportunities because those on welfare are not doing useful work. But, unlike farm subsidies or the other economically destructive transfer programs Congress runs, our welfare program is clearly immoral. Wasting resources that could support something useful like medical research is awful, but to waste resources *and* destroy human dignity in the process is even worse.

Welfare recipients and, what is more frightening, their children do not understand what has happened to them and do not have a clue how to get out. We are trapping people in this horrible system in the name of helping them. This is the least defensible federal policy that exists. It is destroying the lives of millions of people who are victims of the welfare system they are told helps them, while those who pay the bills are becoming ever more resentful about people on welfare. **Politicians play the middle ground—calling for welfare reform, an end to welfare abuse, and for programs that really will help. But all the while they deliver more of the same because they are reelected by doing so.**

Cover Your Eyes

Welfare policy has become an unmentionable. We dance around the issues. Code words and platitudes are used rather than clear language. To imply that people on welfare want to be on welfare is called racist or insensitive. To not be branded racist or insensitive you must agree that even more welfare programs should be provided. What we do not want to admit is that we have created a social monster that is very hard to control. Better to feed the monster a little more every day and hope it does not turn on us than to deal with the problem head on.

We are not helping those on welfare. Many people are on welfare only because they can see no alternative and, in many cases, they do not have the basic skills needed to join the adult working population. They know there is a better world out there, but they are completely divorced from it. **No matter what aspect of the welfare system you look at, the evidence is clear that it encourages irresponsible behavior and produces bad results.**

Most welfare recipients must send their children to the local public school. These schools are well known to be something other than places of learning. The amazing thing is that any child sent to such schools learns anything at all. One study found that only 37% of the black and Hispanic children who entered Chicago public high schools in 1980 graduated. Many of them were really getting a certificate of attendance; of those who graduated, only 21% could read at the proper grade level.

The point is that pouring money into the same awful public schools, which are dealing with many troubled children from no–father families that place little value on education, and do not know what to do about discipline, is not going to work. Some of the worst public schools are the most expensive schools in America. Some of the worst schools in Atlanta cost $11,000 per year per child. People pay less than that to send their kids to fancy private schools. **We need basic reform of the education system, not more money thrown down the same rat hole.**

Another problem identified with low–income people is low–birthweight babies. Low birthweight means higher infant mortality. A Harvard University researcher has shown that the only place this is a serious problem is among unwed mothers. Regardless of race or age, mothers who have babies outside of marriage are less likely to take care of themselves and their babies.

Two-thirds of all black babies and one-fifth of all white babies are now born to unmarried mothers—triple the rate before the "Great Society" showered free medical care on expectant women. Despite great advances in medical care, we have more problems today with low-birthweight babies and infant mortality than we did 30 years ago. **This is the result of a welfare policy that pays unwed women to have babies and reduces their income if they get married.**

Another study by economists at MIT and UCLA found that if poor women participated in all the usual welfare programs—AFDC, food stamps, Medicaid, and public housing—the birthweight of their babies was not improved. There is no reason to think that more welfare—more of the same programs that got us where we are today—is going to improve the situation. Those who are on welfare today are not better off medically than are the poor women who avoid welfare assistance.

Condoms, Anyone?

Instead of dealing head-on with an obvious problem, we see more wasteful, silly ideas take root. One of the latest is the push to pass out birth control information and devices. This will not change behavior. The teenage girls who are getting pregnant know how and why they are getting pregnant. They know as much about sex as those who think they can tell them how to have "responsible" sex.

The problem of sickly babies—who are cared for at great expense by the taxpayers—does not come from a lack of free medical care. It comes from a lack of caring by irresponsible mothers. In our society it is not polite to discuss this. A 700–page report issued in 1991 by the Department of Health and Human Services, called "Healthy People 2000," failed to mention the relationship between low birthweight and illegitimacy. A major study by the Ford Foundation in 1989 about welfare and the future of children never mentioned parental responsibility.

If the government pays some young women to have babies, they will produce them; they are not having children in the course of a normal family relationship. Indeed, **if they enter into a normal family relationship, the government will cut their benefits.** Thus, they are paid to have lots of boyfriends instead of one husband. We are not making a moral judgment about marriage versus illegitimacy; the point is simply that the real–world evidence squares with the common sense belief that children without caring parents is a terrible thing.

Don't Do the Right Thing

We could go on about all the other welfare programs that cause people to behave exactly as we do not want people to behave—unless we like paying the tab for non–working members of society who spend their lives collecting miserable benefits from the government. Politicians are smart people who can see how sick the welfare system is—and that it is causing a segregated America, split between those who are not working and those who resent paying for them. **Members of Congress keep their seats despite having voted for this terrible system, so they are not going to rock the boat.**

Chapter 13

Throw the Rascals Out

It is claimed that the 1992 election will see real change—there will be many new faces in Congress and, whether incumbents win or not, for a while Ross Perot threw a wrench in the political works. **But even if huge numbers of senators and representatives are tossed out, don't expect much change.**

Changing the names in Congress and the White House does not change the system. Every once in a while we have a good sweep in Congress; what has been the result? Remember all the reform–minded "new breed of politician" elected in 1974 after Watergate, or those swept in during the Reagan revolution in 1980? The people elected to office then are now long–term incumbents who have learned to play the political system to keep their seats. The idealistic reformers are now the old guard. On their way to becoming the old guard, they did not change policy much.

Most politicians are not rascals. They are intelligent people responding to the incentives that exist in our political system. Because they want to win—and win again—they do the best job they can of making various special interest groups happy, so campaign funds will be provided to convince a majority of the voters in their state

that they should be kept in office. Our system will not
change by sending pure–hearted people to Washington or to
the state capitol. Many politicians are pure–hearted and
have good ideas, but they do what they do to survive and
get reelected. **Changing the people in office will not make
much difference; changing the system will.**

Do the Right Thing

Regardless of political views, all would agree that we
want government to perform its functions fairly and
efficiently. People may disagree about the best way to
reform welfare, Social Security, health care, foreign aid,
and other problems that demand attention, but there is broad
agreement that reform is needed. **Significant reform is not
going to come from people who are politically successful
by patching together a quilt of special interest legislation, subsidies, and other goodies that bundles the
whole inefficient mess together.**

Opinion surveys consistently show that taxpayers are
willing to pay taxes to help the poor, to provide quality
schools, to build good roads, to clean the environment, and
to do other things that improve society. What voters do not
like is the fact that huge amounts of tax dollars are wasted
in almost everything the government does. And even if a
politician wants to do the right thing, the system is biased
against meaningful reform.

Outsiders: Symbols, Not Solutions

The support expressed for Ross Perot was a sign that
people are fed up with the mess our political system has
made of our government. Almost no one knew what Perot
stood for on most issues. The point is that people did not
care what Perot's solutions were supposed to be. For years,

candidates have promised one thing during their campaigns and then done something else. **Read their lips: Perot was a symbol of voter frustration—an outsider. People want change because the Bill Clintons and George Bushes of the political world are not solving the problems.**

The insiders, the people who know how to work in the political system, were opposed to Perot. When *Fortune* magazine polled the chief executive officers of large corporations in May, only 11% supported Perot; 78% favored President Bush. Contrast that to a May survey of the chief executives of small, fast–growing companies; 43% supported Perot and 40% supported Bush. It is not that the heads of the big corporations think everything is great in America, but they know how to work in the system as it is now. Perot threatened the established political order.

But even if Ross Perot was the smartest person ever to be in presidential politics, alone he would have made little difference. The reason is that members of Congress will not cut their own political throats to help any president. **Our country would be much better served by elected officials who will take courageous stands and who are not afraid to upset the apple cart because they are not worried about saving their own political hides.**

It's Politics, Not Party

When Jimmy Carter was elected president, he looked at the budget mess then, which looks like a pittance today, and he put out a "hit list" of wasteful government spending programs that had to be cut to get spending under control. Who stopped him in his tracks? The Democrat–controlled Congress that was supposed to be happy to have one of its own in the White House. The Democratic party could not produce reform even when the head of the party sat in the White House and its members ran Congress. Party platforms are shams; politicians ignore them and voters cannot rely on them.

When Ronald Reagan was elected in 1980, Republicans took control of the Senate and nearly had control of the House. Again, efforts by a president to control spending and impose real reform were derailed by some self–serving members of the same political party. Let's look at one story that is typical of what happens when an effort to reform government and control spending is made.

Can't Touch That

The 1980 election was hailed as a watershed political year. The anti–government sentiment gave the Republicans their biggest vote in years and made a lot of Democrats *talk* about controlling big government. Reagan appointed some serious reformers to various offices who wanted to control spending and regulations. That meant cutting budgets and firing some government employees. Hard choices had to be made; but the 1980 election told politicians that such choices were what the voters wanted.

President Reagan appointed James C. Miller as Chairman of the Federal Trade Commission (FTC). For budget year 1981 Congress had allocated $70.8 million to the FTC. For budget year 1982, Mr. Miller requested $61.1 million, a 13.7% budget cut from the year before. Did Congress thank this agency head for doing a good job? No. To put it mildly, Congress had a fit. A long battle followed and Congress forced the FTC to take $68.8 million, a budget cut of less than 3%. That is, the bureaucrats were forced to accept a much bigger budget than they said they needed to do the job. The same thing happened in 1983 and 1984; Congress gave the agency more money than it requested.

The FTC is a drop in the government bucket. But this story is not unique—the same thing happened at many other agencies. **It does not matter what federal agency or program is at stake—the Department of Justice or the Split Hair Ends Commission—they all mean power and control to Congress.**

Why was the FTC not allowed to cut its budget? Because it meant that the members of Congress on the House and Senate committees that give that agency its orders would have less to control. At a smaller agency, there would be fewer favors Congress could order done for various special interests that want intervention at the agency on their behalf. Members of Congress may be happy to see the budget cut in areas over which they have no say, but when *their* turf is threatened they fight to keep it.

Other members of Congress were incensed that there would be cuts in staff jobs at various FTC offices around the country. Most senators and representatives could care less about the FTC, but they care about any federal job in their state, so the effort to close various FTC offices was stopped.

Suppose Congress had cut the budget of the FTC. Who would have noticed? Would ordinary voters have known about this drop in the bucket being saved? Of course not; voters only see general trends and hear bits of news. It is impossible for voters to know the details of what goes on in Washington. But if the FTC had been made smaller, a few federal jobs would have been cut. The people who lost their jobs—and their friends and family—would blame their senator or representative for allowing this to happen. **There is little political gain but a lot of political loss to the member of Congress who supports budget cuts.**

Bring Home the Bacon

This process is not a matter of liberal versus conservative or Republican versus Democrat; it is reelection

politics. To maximize the chance of reelection, members of Congress fight to have as much control over the parts of the government they can influence, and fight for as many federal goodies for their districts as they can.

The cost of one more federal boondoggle in one state is covered by taxpayers spread all over the nation—no one takes the blame for the cost of a program buried in a $1.5 trillion budget. But the benefits are seen in the state where a member of Congress can claim credit. The costs and benefits for the nation may be horrendous, but they look good from the viewpoint of each member of Congress who wants to make the home folks happy. **Our political system encourages members of Congress to act selfishly, not to think about the good of the nation.**

A senator or representative who votes against all special interest goodies, that every other member of Congress wants, will get nothing to take home. Every state and congressional district pays federal taxes. Those taxes go into one big pie that Congress gets to cut. The money may go for national defense, highways, toxic waste cleanup, or parks, but Congress (with some help from the White House) decides if the money is spent in Texas or one of the other 49 states.

Your representative either gets in there and fights for your share of the pie while it is being cut, or you just pay for the pie that gets eaten in 434 other congressional districts and you get nothing. All members of Congress are trapped by the system. If they vote against wasteful projects there is no savings for their voters—the home folks save nothing and get nothing. So all voters should want their senators and representatives to be skillful political infighters; if they are, leave them in Washington forever.

Consider the authors' state of South Carolina. Strom Thurmond, a Republican, has been in the Senate for 38 years. Fritz Hollings, a Democrat, has been in the Senate for 26 years. Both are known to be skillful legislators who fight for their state. In 1990, South Carolina residents paid 1.03% of the total federal tax bill, but got back 1.36% of all federal spending. We got $2.9 billion more in federal benefits than we paid in taxes. We appreciate your support.

Strom Thurmond and Fritz Hollings are considered to be pretty conservative. We have no doubt that they believe in fiscal responsibility. But they have not had long careers in Washington by sitting back and wailing about fiscal insanity—they get in there and fight for every nickel. If they did not, the voters of South Carolina *should* vote them out and send someone who can bring home the bacon. Other members of Congress will not cut South Carolina's federal taxes if it gets fewer benefits.

Going To Have a Revolution

Name all the countries where the government was overthrown because the citizens were mad that they were not paying enough taxes or because the government was not large enough. It is a pretty short list. Obviously, people get fed up with governments when they impose too many taxes, especially when there is nothing much in return.

There does not have to be a Russian revolution, tossing out the whole government, in order to have reform. Sweden, one of the most highly taxed democratic countries in the world, is having a quiet revolution. A new government is cutting spending on welfare; it has started parental choice in education; and it is engaged in wholesale reform of government programs that had stifled life and economic growth in that country.

In the mid–80s the same thing happened in New Zealand. A new government tossed out every farm subsidy and many other economically destructive programs that had taken New Zealand from one of the highest income levels in the world to an also–ran. The adjustment was tough, but after years of no growth, New Zealand's economy boomed. **If change for the better can happen peacefully in democratic nations such as Sweden and New Zealand, why do we not get it here?**

In this book, we have been critical of many government programs. Almost everyone knows that the goals of most government programs could be achieved more efficiently and effectively than they are now. Exactly how we should reform various programs is irrelevant—they are not going to be reformed unless politicians have different incentives.

Analysts of all political stripes have proposed sensible reforms that would make government programs work better. Some think we should spend more, some think we should spend less, but all agree that we could get where we want to go more efficiently. This is nothing new. Congress has always been bombarded with sensible information by its own staff, bureaucrats, and independent outsiders about how to improve things. **In our political system, Congress cannot adopt reforms unless it is sure the benefits will be greater than the cost—*for members of Congress*. Their primary concern is reelection to their jobs, not the welfare of the nation.**

If It's Broke, Fix It

Some people think the problem with the American government is that we do not have brilliant people in Washington the way we did in the good old days. In olden times we had, among the luminaries, Thomas Jefferson, Daniel Webster, and John C. Calhoun. There is no question but that they were tremendous intellects. But we have people in politics just as intelligent today. The main difference is that **in the 1800s the Congress had control over very few resources; today, directly or indirectly, it**

directs half of the nation's output. In days of yore members of Congress could think about great issues; today they hardly have time to think about a billion here and a billion there. **The problem in government today is not the people, it's the system. Our elected officials do not have the right incentives.**

Term limitation will play a key role in making government responsive to the needs of the times. We do not know if it will make government bigger or smaller, but we believe it will make our representatives more independent of special interests and more likely to respond to the desires of ordinary citizens. **Those who have slurped at the public trough for too long do not want term limits. Special interest groups know how to milk the system at taxpayer expense.** Even though the chase for federal goodies has ground economic growth to a stop, the special interests have theirs, so they do not want to rock the boat.

In the next chapter we will explain how term limits will change the nature of our system. Under term limits, the people who go to Washington may be the same folks, but their incentives will be different. To those who say the system ain't broke, so don't fix it, we say they, the critics, are the reason it is broke. The criticisms of term limits will be answered point by point.

Chapter 14

Why Term Limits?

We have seen how the current political system promotes special interests, increases wasteful government spending, and perpetuates bad programs. From January 1, 1991, to March 31, 1992, incumbents in Congress raked in 97% of the $73 million passed out by Political Action Committees. **Incumbents get large donations from special interest groups so they will leave things as they are or will deliver more goodies. They do not get donations to work for substantive reform that means kicking special interests in the teeth.**

Many members of Congress know why we are in an economic mess, and what needs to be done to get out of it. But few people who have successful political careers are going to put the interest of the nation before their personal self–interest, which allows them to spend their lives in Congress.

I Got Mine

You know your enemies by the company they keep. Who funds the opposition to term limits? In 1991, a term limits initiative was on the ballot in Washington state. With senior members of Congress such as House Speaker Tom Foley facing the prospect of losing their seats, the special interests—big business and big labor—rushed to fund the campaign to *defeat* term limits. Labor unions kicked in $50,000. Cigarette–maker Philip Morris tossed in $25,000; and $10,000 or more came from Kaiser Aluminum, Boeing Aircraft, the National Rifle Association, and the Association of Trial Lawyers of America.

None of these organizations, diverse as they are, loves every member of Congress from Washington state or from any other state, but all special interests are afraid of the changes that term limits will bring. Special interests, which have invested in expensive Washington operations, know how to work with Congress as it is structured now. **Term limits means the special interests will have a hard time having long–term cozy relations with members of Congress.**

While opposition to term limits by big business and big labor is strong evidence that there must be something right about term limits, let's consider the serious arguments raised against term limits.

It's Not Democratic

Term limits means that elected officials must leave office after a certain time, regardless of how popular they are. This is attacked as anti–democratic; we should be free to select whoever we want to elect to office, the argument goes. The response to this has two parts: (1) There is nothing democratic about elected officials who can exploit their office to make sure that they will probably never lose their seats; and (2) restrictions on who may be in office are in fact actually quite common.

Members of Congress have power over federal government resources that challengers do not. Incumbents do

favors for constituents and special interests that generate
campaign support and votes that a challenger cannot even
begin to match. There is nothing "fair" about races for
Congress—incumbents generate support by exploiting the
powers of office. Challengers can only make *claims* about
doing something different.

Our Constitution, like any constitution, sets the terms
and conditions of office. You may not be elected president
of the United States unless you were born in the United
States. Even if a majority of the voters wanted former
British Prime Minister Margaret Thatcher to be president,
she could not be elected. You also have to be at least 35
years old to be president. Even if a majority of the voters
wanted Michael Jordan to be president, instead of playing
basketball for the Chicago Bulls, he could not be elected.
And we have term limits for the president (adopted after
Franklin Roosevelt's four terms) as well as for governors of
most states. Restricting who may be in office—and for how
long—is an American tradition.

Free to Choose

Harvard economist Robert Barro argues that term limits
is a bad idea because it would restrict competition in the
political market. He says that we do not want government
to tell us that we must use a new brand of toothpaste
because we have been using a familiar brand such as Crest
for too long; similarly, we do not want the government to
tell us we must elect new representatives because we have
been electing familiar politicians for too long.

We would agree with this argument if politicians
operated in freely competitive markets. Members of
Congress do not, though; they are monopolists. They have
political power and resources provided at *taxpayer* expense.
Over 30,000 people work for Congress itself—that is, more

than 50 staff people per senator and representative. The budget of Congress itself is now $2.5 billion per year, or $5 million *per member* of Congress.

Complaints about Congressional salaries are misplaced. The pay earned by members of Congress is a drop in the bucket compared to the huge expense of running congressional offices. Many members of Congress spend more on postage mailing advertisements about themselves (at taxpayer expense) than they get in salary. **Members of Congress have a built–in political machine, paid for by taxpayers, that works to keep them in Congress.**

Add to this machine the power of congressional office to draw campaign help from special interests, and it is clear why it is so hard to knock an incumbent out of office. When Al Gore ran for reelection to the Senate in 1990, he raised over $2.6 million, including $1.2 million from political action committees. His opponent had $6,510. The deck is stacked in favor of incumbents, which is why in recent years only 2 to 3% of the incumbents running for reelection to the House were defeated.

There is no "level playing field" in running for Congress. A new candidate runs against the power of Congress, not just against an incumbent. This is not Crest toothpaste versus a new brand of toothpaste; this is Crest with advertising paid by taxpayers blowing away challengers who have the cards stacked against them when they try to raise money to offer another brand.

Government is fundamentally different from private markets. We can all walk away from private markets. The makers of Crest toothpaste may be successful, but they did it on their own. If you don't like Crest, don't buy it. You can ignore IBM or General Motors; they cannot force you to buy anything. But you cannot easily walk away from the United States government if you do not like what it supplies. Unless you want to risk going to jail, you must pay for what the government says you will support as a taxpayer. **The force that goes with government authority means that we must have rules in place that keep those we elect from becoming those who dictate to us.**

Bureaucrats Will Take Over

Some critics of term limits claim that without long–time legislators in Congress no one will be able to control the bureaucrats. They assert that with term limits, short–time members of Congress will be too inexperienced to deal with clever bureaucrats who will then run the show, leaving us worse off than before.

This argument fails for several reasons. As we discussed before, bureaucrats work for Congress and the president. This is a straightforward legal relationship. **Congress and the president have the power to reduce the size and power of government agencies any time they want to pass legislation to do so.** Of course bureaucrats want more money and power for their agencies, but that does not happen without direct approval by their bosses in Congress.

It is convenient for members of Congress to make bureaucrats a whipping boy. Politicians like to talk as if they are needed to keep bureaucrats in line, when they already have them under control. Earlier we discussed examples of bureaucrats making good–faith budget requests, only to have Congress force special interest spending on bureaucracies, reducing their effectiveness. Bureaucrats are decent Americans who happen to work for government; they are not evil beings who sit around thinking about how to hurt the country by wasting money.

Bureaucracies continue to grow and become more powerful because Congress wants that to happen. Bureaucracies are a necessary part of government. Since bureaucrats know what members of Congress want, it is in their

interest to offer suggestions and help to Congress about
how to get goodies delivered where Congress wants them
to go. There is nothing wrong with this. **What is wrong
are the relationships built up between bureaucracies and
long–term members of Congress.**

For example, Representative John Dingell, chairman of
the Energy and Commerce Committee, who has been in
Congress since 1955, not only has a huge staff of his own
but has 22 employees of the Government Accounting Office
detailed to his office. The 16 Republicans on the Energy
and Commerce Committee have none.

Obviously, long terms in Congress mean power. A part
of this power is a close working relationship with bureaucracies. Term limits will mean that members of Congress
will have little reason or ability to develop cozy deals with
bureaucracies. It is hardly democratic for long–term
members of Congress to have more power than short–term
members. **Term limits will help break the power of the
congressional committee heads who set the agenda and
will allow more open consideration of fresh policies.**

As we saw in Chapter 2, on average, the longer people
are in Congress, the more they become big spenders. That
is, the biggest backers of more bureaucracy are old–timers
in Congress who know how to play the system and run the
committees. To say that experienced legislators are keeping
the bureaucrats under control simply does not square with
the facts presented by voting records. **Long–term members
of Congress from both parties vote for more bureaucracy than do members who have been in office for
shorter times.**

Change Policies

Finally, the critics of term limits say that if you are not
happy with the way things are working, tell your represen-

tatives to change the policies to make things better. This argument has the least merit of all. As we have discussed many times, members of Congress are well informed about policy alternatives. They have the power to change the things over which they weep crocodile tears, but they will not force real reform because they keep their seats by doing what they do now.

We have been in the economic doldrums for two decades because of political gridlock. Senators and representatives know this better than anyone. They are smart people who know about the problems and are well informed about reform alternatives. But when problems happen, what do we get? More of the same rag–tag special interest politics.

Think of all the hand–wringing and pious statements made by politicians after the 1992 Los Angeles riots. They said we must do something about the urban areas that are economic and social blights. What do we get out of Congress? An "urban aid" bill that is a joke; it includes provisions about such things as taxes on yachts and jewelry. As Senator Bill Bradley said, this is not "a meaningful urban–aid package, but...tax breaks for a bunch of special interests." Housing Secretary Jack Kemp agreed that the bill is a "message to Los Angeles and low–income people everywhere to drop dead."

We do not know if more government spending on urban areas is a good idea or not. The point is that no matter what the issue, it's politics as usual. There is no chance for meaningful reform legislation—conservative or liberal—to pass. This is *not* because we have sent the wrong people to Washington; it is because the major concern of members of Congress is reelection. **The easiest way to get reelected is to pass out goodies to special interest groups that grease the election skids.**

Why Limits

Those who see nothing wrong with a zero–growth economy and an ever–growing government will not be interested in term limits. Term limits will change the nature of our political system so that policies can be implemented that will encourage, or at least not discourage, economic prosperity. Term limits will change the nature of political relationships so that special interests will play a smaller role, political independence will increase, and party platforms will become more meaningful.

Term limits will force those who make laws to live under the laws they pass because they will become normal citizens again. Congress now passes laws that it *does not apply to itself.* After all, most senators and representatives intend to spend their lives in the rarefied air of Congress—not among the people on whom they impose laws. **Members of Congress want to govern but not be governed.** Term limits means we will have more citizen–legislators who will not spend their lives in Washington. After a stint in Congress, most will return to work and live in Los Angeles, Detroit, Orlando, or whatever part of the country they represented. The virtue of this is not a new idea. **Aristotle said that the key to democracy is in "ruling and being ruled in turn."**

The founders of this nation considered including term limits in the Constitution but did not because, in large part, they could not imagine that anyone would want to make a life in Washington politics. Government was important but small; service was a duty, not a way to make a profitable career. Furthermore, until 1914, Senators were appointed by state legislatures, so election was only an issue for members of the House.

Nevertheless, many of the founders recognized that not having term limits was a mistake. Thomas Jefferson said "I dislike, and greatly dislike [in the new Constitution] the abandonment in every instance of the principle of rotation in office." His thoughts were seconded by George Washington who said, "A rotation of elected officers [may be] most congenial with the ideas [the people have] of liberty and safety." **Washington and Jefferson, being men of great integrity, quit the presidency after two terms because they feared the effects of a lifetime in office.**

How It Will Work

Term limits will change the incentives of politicians and the structure of the American political system. The most important effect will be on the incentives of senators and representatives. A person who knows that he or she cannot make a career out of being in Congress will worry less about losing an election. After all, losing just means a quicker return home, which was coming anyway, not the end of an anticipated lifetime in Washington.

With term limits, members of Congress would be less concerned about building large campaign war chests from special interest groups because the personal cost of not being reelected would be quite small. Special interest support would still be available, but many of the good people we send to Washington would be much less likely to be sucked into the game of endlessly satisfying established well–financed interests. **Term limits will make it very difficult to put together long–term cozy deals in an "old boys" club.**

Term limits, as generally understood, means that the longest stint in the House would be three or four terms (6 or 8 years) and two terms (12 years) in the Senate. A majority of members would change every 4 years in the House and every 6 years in the Senate. Because many members of Congress would, by definition, be in their last term, they would have little reason to care about satisfying the interests of those who hold out promises of campaign support. Members of Congress could do what they thought was right and not be as concerned about antagonizing some special interest group.

Make Politics Matter

Politics is a dirty word in America; it has come to mean politicians feeding special interests while telling half–truths to the public. But politics is serious business; it is about the governance of a nation. The political process determines the rules we must live under and, given the size of government, determines how much economic growth we will be allowed to enjoy.

Party labels have come to mean little; politicians simply do whatever it takes to get reelected forever. Many good people are forced to give in to special interests that other members of Congress serve, in order to get support for the goodies their constituents and special interests want. They do this to garner the support needed for reelection. Every state has special interests and, as individuals, we all support various special interests, but serving special interests has become the end–all of our political process. Every bit of legislation, such as urban aid, is an opportunity to tack on special interest trinkets. Republicans and Democrats all play the same game. **The only way to limit the self interest of politicians to indulge special interests is to limit their ability to be reelected.**

The Rise of Political Parties

Term limits means that individual politicians will matter less; party labels will matter more. Because senators and representatives will turn over in office frequently, voters will know less about individual candidates, and incumbents will *not* have huge war chests for campaigns paid for by special interest groups. Because individual politicians will matter less and not have life tenure, political parties will take more responsibility for providing the mechanism necessary to get new faces elected. Being a Democrat or a Republican or some other party will mean more than it used to.

Political parties will stake out positions and back candidates who will be expected to follow the party platform. Parties will be much more important sources of financial, technical, and voter support than they are now. Currently, the best strategy for voters is to support incumbents and forget about policy positions. The power of incumbency is important to the delivery of a share of the favors Congress distributes.

As it stands now, incumbents have so much power they can pretty much ignore the party to which they belong. This reduces their commitment to stand by party platforms. A party may call for, say, a balanced budget, but members of the party can ignore the platform and vote to bust the budget. With limited terms, party discipline will be more effective because a party label will come to mean more to voters than the names of the candidates, whom voters will often not recognize.

Hence, American politics will become more like politics in England and other countries, where people vote more for the issues staked out by parties than for individuals. **We will benefit from having politicians who are closer to party platforms, not individual incumbents who only work to provide goodies at others' expense.**

If a party has control and delivers the policies it promised, it is likely to be rewarded by more voters' support of its candidates for Congress. If the party has control and does not do what it says, it will have little excuse; and many of its candidates will lose elections together. This forces more discipline along party lines—members of Congress must vote for the policies they were elected to put in place or they face the prospect of being turned out by their own party in the primary, or being tossed out with other party members who failed to deliver what was promised.

This does not mean that members of Congress will become talking heads for their parties without their own thoughts. There will be serious discussions within parties about what platform to put forward to impress the voters. It will be in the interest of members of Congress, who usually are strong-willed people with a sincere interest in policy matters, to fight for a policy that will help the party win control of Congress, and then to stick by it if elected.

Only by this mechanism can rapid political reform occur. It happened in England. Margaret Thatcher led the Conservative party to success over the Labour party because her party staked out a clear platform; Conservatives stayed in power because they delivered a lot of what was promised. There were major changes in British policies. The voters were offered clear alternatives in party policies and they know the parties will generally deliver what they say they will. **With term limits, voters will have a much better chance of effecting real policy changes than under the current system, in which politicians are independent operators mostly concerned about their own election, principles be damned.**

Govern and Be Governed

Benjamin Franklin noted that "In free governments, the rulers are the servants, and the people their superiors.... For the former, to return among the latter [does] not degrade, but promote them." This is the major reason for term limits.

When politicians know they must return to ordinary society and live under the laws passed while they are in Congress, they will think more carefully about the long–term effects of the programs they support. Their end–all will not be reelection, because that option will not be available. Their end–all will be to live the rest of their lives as American citizens.

Chapter 15

Term Limits Are Happening!

Breaking the political gridlock that has forced our economy into two decades of doldrums requires strong action. Americans are fed up with politics and politicians. People are cynical; most believe that "the system" is so rotten that we need a fundamental restructuring of our institutions. The sense that "the people" have is correct; we need basic reform.

Politicians sense this, too. Bill Clinton tried to stir interest by calling for "A New Covenant," but failed to explain what he was talking about that was really new. Ross Perot obviously understood the frustration; but he did not call for anything new, except to dump the Republican and Democratic candidates in favor of an outsider who promised to do things differently. George Bush, who is somewhat a victim of forces beyond his control, appeared unable to comprehend or vocalize the kind of reform needed.

There is nothing particularly wrong with Clinton or Bush. There is nothing particularly wrong with most of the people in Congress. What is wrong are the incentives faced by politicians to make careers out of politics. The main

problem is with our Congress and, more and more, our state
legislatures. **Most legislators are career politicians who
get reelected for life by delivering what special interests
want.** Gridlock in government has been brought on by the
dominance of special interests in the legislatures.

Put the Welfare of the Nation First

Presidents usually have had more sense than Congress;
not because the men who have been in that office are
smarter than members of Congress, but because presidents
know that their end of political office is in sight. At most
they have two terms. While they have party politics to think
about, they also understand that there are no more offices
for them. They can think about governing the country and
changing things for the better. Being human, presidents
make mistakes. But it is clear that because they know they
have a limited time in office, they want to be remembered
for having done some good things, not for having been paid
off by umpteen special interests they need to fund their
reelection efforts.

   **Term limits is a necessary step to change the incen-
tives of members of Congress to think more about the
good of the country and less about their next campaign.**
Term limits is *structural reform* that will help provide
incentives for politicians more in keeping with what we
want representatives in a democracy to be like—people who
will govern and then return to live in the society they
helped to govern. **Only people with no political future
can have the political courage to undertake reforms that
will tell special interests that there will be fewer goodies.**
No more taking from Peter, or Peter's children, to pay Paul.

   Term limits is not the cure–all for gridlock in government and in the economy. But it is a necessary step to
reforms that will take decades to undo the damage that has

been already done. As we have seen, perpetual budget deficits, the growing national debt, and, even more, the Social Security debt are monsters. But we can pay these bills—our elected representatives promised people certain benefits and we should live up to our promises. We can have needed government services that most people want. But for these things to be affordable, we have to get the economy growing.

Economic growth means higher standards of living, less poverty, and more tax revenues without higher tax *rates* to cover the bills that have piled up. **Economic growth will not occur when politicians who *punish* economic success are in charge.** We must reward the saving, investment, and productive behavior that will provide the resources to get us out of our no–growth economy. Understanding this does not require genius; politicians know that government must get out of the way for economic growth to occur. It does not happen now because politicians' incentives are the opposite of what they need to be. Currently they are rewarded with long careers in office by controlling more and more of the private sector. **Term limits will allow politicians to connect their legislative actions to their understanding of the issues, not their understanding of campaign resources.**

What's Happening

The term–limits movement is a grass–roots movement. In contrast, most so–called "reform" movements have behind them some special interest group that will benefit by the change. Term limits is supported by, among others, some wealthy people, but there is no evidence of special interests being behind the movement. Its support is broad–based; it is liberal and conservative. It is something that a lot of people have decided must be done to help break gridlock in government.

Most would trace the current movement to 1989, when state senator Terry Considine of Colorado joined with friends to found Coloradans Back in Charge. Considine introduced term–limits legislation in the Colorado legislature, but it got nowhere. The group then collected voter signatures to put a term limits initiative on the 1990 Colorado ballot, which 71% of the voters supported. Now in Colorado, members of Congress are limited to 12 years in the House or in the Senate; members of the state legislature are limited to two four–year terms (8 years) in the senate and to four two–year terms (8 years) in the house.

At the same time the effort was moving forward in Colorado, voters in Oklahoma put a term–limits initiative on the 1990 ballot; in that election, 67% of the Oklahoma voters supported the initiative to limit the terms of members of the state legislature to 12 years in either house. The same year, voters in California supported an initiative to limit the terms of legislators to 8 years in the state senate and 6 years in the state house. That new law was challenged, but was upheld as constitutional by the Supreme Court of California.

The only term–limits loss has been in Washington state. In the 1991 election, the initiative was defeated 46% to 54%. The loss was attributed to the big–money campaign mounted against the initiative and to the fact that voters were aware that Washington would be hurt if it was the only state to have *retroactive* term limits. That is, because current members of Congress would have to count the years already in office against their limits, the Washington state delegation would be cleaned out in a few years, leaving Washington state with no senior people in a Congress full of members facing no term limits. The measure is expected to be back on the ballot this year, but the new term limits law would not count past years of service against incumbent members of Congress.

Term limits have been imposed on city officials in place in Houston, San Antonio, Kansas City, Wichita, Jacksonville, New Orleans, Colorado Springs, and other cities. In most cases, the initiatives on the ballot have been approved by huge majorities, just as polls around the country consistently show high levels of popular support for limits.

Prospects for 1992

The following term limits for Congress are expected to be on the ballot in November of 1992:

12–year limit in the House and Senate
North Dakota
South Dakota

**8–year limit in the House
& 12–year limit in the Senate**
Florida
Missouri
Ohio
Nebraska

**6–year limit in the House
& 12–year limit in the Senate**
Arizona
Arkansas
California
Michigan
Montana
Nevada
Oregon
Washington
Wyoming

It is possible that after the 1992 elections almost one–third of the states will have adopted term limits. In most states, initiatives on the ballot limit the terms of members of the state legislature and of members of Congress. While term limits began as 12–year limits in either the House or the Senate, most people agree that 12 years in the House is too long—that means 5 reelections because they run every two years. Therefore, most states are looking at 6–year limits in the House (three two–year terms) and 12–year limits in the Senate (two six–year terms). In most states, members of the state legislatures would be limited to 8 years in either house of the legislature.

In most cases, the same limits would apply to members of the state legislature. The language of the initiative on the ballot in Oregon illustrates how term limits can be written into a state constitution. It follows:

AN ACT

Paragraph 1. TERM LIMITS. The Constitution of the State of Oregon is amended by creating new Sections 19 and 20 in Article II, to read:

SECTION 19. Limits on Oregon Terms. To promote varied representation, to broaden the opportunities for public service, and to make the electoral process fairer by reducing the power of incumbency, terms in Oregon elected offices are limited as follows:

(1) No person shall serve more than six years in the Oregon House of Representatives, eight years in the Oregon Senate, and twelve years in the Oregon Legislature in his or her lifetime.

(2) No person shall serve more than eight years in each Oregon statewide office in his or her lifetime.

(3) Only terms of service beginning after this Act goes into effect shall count towards the limits of this Section.

(4) When a person is appointed or elected to fill a vacancy in office, then such service shall be counted as one term for the purposes of this Section.

(5) A person shall not appear on the ballot as a candidate for elected office or be appointed to fill a vacancy in office if serving a full term in such office would cause him or her to violate the limits in this Section.

(6) This Section does not apply to judicial officials.

SECTION 20. Limits on Congressional Terms. To promote varied representation, to broaden the opportunities for public service, and to make the electoral process fairer by reducing the power of incumbency. Terms in the United States Congress representing Oregon are limited as follows:

(1) No person shall represent Oregon for more than six years in the U.S. House of Representatives and twelve years in the U.S. Senate in his or her lifetime.

(2) Only terms of service beginning after this Act goes into effect shall count towards the limits of this Section.

(3) When a person is appointed or elected to fill a vacancy in office, then such service shall be counted as one term for the purposes of this Section.

(4) A person shall not appear on the ballot as a candidate for elected office or be appointed to fill a vacancy in office if serving a full term in such office would cause him or her to violate the limits in this Section.

(The rest of the initiative has to do with procedural details. If you want to know more about the details of term limit activities in various states, you can contact one of the organizations listed in the Data Sources for Chapter 15.)

If initiatives like this pass in all states there will be 16 states with term limits. One-third of the members of the House and the Senate would be under term limits. A push for an amendment to the U.S. Constitution to limit terms would be likely. This would make sure that some states do not take advantage of the states that impose limits on their

representatives. There is concern that if some states do not
limit terms, and send their senators and representatives to
Washington forever, they may gain extra benefits at the
expense of the states with limits. However, members of
Congress from states with term limits are unlikely to
support the seniority system in Congress, so the advantages
of lifetime reelection would be greatly reduced.

Take the Pledge

Term limits is on the ballot in most states in which
citizens have the power to put the measure on the ballot.
Initiatives may be used in future elections in Alaska, Idaho,
Maine and Utah. In all other states, the legislature must act.
It should come as no surprise that the measure is not on the
ballot in non–initiative states—legislators do not want to
put on the ballot a popular measure that would limit their
terms in office.

By the nature of representative government, we cannot
force legislators to vote in favor of something they do not
want. We can, however, ask political candidates if they
would vote specifically for something, so they are on record
on the issue. In many states, candidates for the state
legislature are being asked to sign a pledge that they will
support a constitutional amendment in the legislature to
impose term limits on members of the legislature and on
the state's Washington, D.C., delegation. While they can
break their pledge, no one likes a liar and most politicians
do not want to be caught in a flat–out lie.

Term limits will be introduced in many state legislatures
during the coming year. In many states, legislators are
helping to force the issue, so the public can know the
position of all legislators. If members of the legislature will
not vote to limit legislative terms, voters can quickly limit
their terms of office at the next election. Massachusetts

Governor Weld, Minnesota Governor Carlson, Rhode Island Governor Sundlun, Texas Governor Richards, and other political leaders have also endorsed term limits. **Term limits is bi-partisan reform that will allow meaningful change to take place at the state and federal level.**

For the Next Generation

Environmentalists often make the point that we have a duty not to leave an environmental mess behind for the next generation to clean up. Our theme in this book has been that we are in an economic mess that is leaving a huge bill for the next generation to pay. To do so is not right. It violates any decent person's sense of fairness. **We have created this economic mess by politics that are polluted with special interest dominance.** Legislators must contribute to this gridlock or lose special interest support and then lose their office. Term limits will give the next generation of politicians the incentive to work for the good of the citizens who elect them. Give term limits a chance. Our children deserve a better future.

DATA SOURCES

Sources are listed only the first time they are used.

Chapter 2:
Michael Barone and Grant Ujifusa, *The Almanac of American Politics 1992*, Washington: National Journal, 1992.
"Congress, My Congressman," *American Enterprise*, May/June 1992, p. 102.
Tom Miller, *Competitive Enterprise Index: 101st Congress, 1989*, Washington: Competitive Enterprise Institute, 1990.
James L. Payne, *The Culture of Spending*, San Francisco: ICS Press, 1991.
James L. Payne, "Bad Influence," *Reason*, Aug./Sept. 1991, p. 42.

Chapter 3:
"A Privileged Class," *Wall Street Journal*, March 11, 1992.
"Congressional Bureaucracy," *Executive Alert*, Dallas: National Center for Policy Analysis, Jan./Feb. 1992.
Economic Report of the President, 1992.
Historical Statistics of the United States: Colonial Times to 1957, Washington: U.S. GPO, 1971.
Scott Hodge, ed., *A Prosperity Plan for America*, Washington: Heritage Foundation, 1992.
Scott Hodge and Robert Rector, "What George Bush Is Not Being Told About Federal Spending," Backgrounder No. 886, Washington: Heritage Foundation, March 1992.
Social Security Bulletin: Annual Statistical Supplement, 1991.
Statistical Abstract of the United States, 1991.
Stephen Moore, "State Spending Splurge," Policy Analysis No. 152, Washington: Cato Institute, May 1991.

Chapter 4:
"Federal Regulations to Prevent Infection Of Health-Care Workers Will Be Costly," *Wall Street Journal*, July 2, 1992, p. B1.
Steve Hanke and Stephen Walters, *Social Regulation: A Report Card*, Washington: National Chamber Foundation, 1990.
Hopkins, Thomas D., *The Costs of Federal Regulation*, Washington: National Chamber Foundation, 1992.
"Today's U.S. Worker," *Fortune*, May 4, 1992, p. 60.
Melinda Warren, *Regulation on the Rise: Analysis of the Federal Budget for 1992*, St. Louis: Center for the Study of American Business, 1991.

"What Happened to the American Dream?" *Business Week*, August 19, 1991, p. 80.

Chapter 5:
"Attention Refocuses on U.S. Courtship of Iraq," *Wall Street Journal*, May 12, 1992, p. A18.
"Federal Subsidies Flow To Rural Phone Firms That Have Lots of Cash," *Wall Street Journal*, May 23, 1991, p. A1.
"First Family of Sugar Is Tough on Workers, Generous to Politicians," *Wall Street Journal*, July 29, 1991, p. A1.
"General Aspin's Pork Army," *Wall Street Journal*, May 21, 1991, p. A22.
"Law Forces Pentagon to Purchase and Store Metal It Doesn't Want," *Wall Street Journal*, June 10, 1991, p. A1.
"Pork Barrel 'Science'," *Science*, December 6, 1991, p. 1433.
"Privatize the World Bank," *Wall Street Journal*, May 17, 1991, p. A14.
Spotlight on Congress, Washington: Free Congress Foundation, various issues, 1991.

Chapter 6:
Rick Henderson, "Spending Spree," *Reason*, Feb. 1992, p. 17.
"House Narrowly Defeats Amendment To Constitution on Balancing Budget," *Wall Street Journal*, June 12, 1992, p. A2.
"How Balanced-Budget Amendment Traveled From Certain To Sunk," *Bozeman [MT] Daily Chronicle*, July 6, 1992, p. 6.
Daniel Mitchell, "Bring Back Gramm-Rudman," *Wall Street Journal*, Aug. 12, 1991, p. A10.
"Proposal for Balanced-Budget Amendment Moves To Front Burner as Lawmakers Hunt for an Issue," *Wall Street Journal*, May 13, 1992, p. A18.
Lewis K. Uhler, *Setting Limits*, Washington: Regnery Gateway, 1989.
Mark Wheat and David Beers, "Red Ink at High Tide, Low Ebb for Accountability," *Issues and Answers*, Washington: Citizens for a Sound Economy Foundation, August 28, 1991.

Chapter 7:
Alan Greenspan, "Statement to the Deficit Commission," *The Federal Reserve Bulletin*, January 1989.
Laurence J. Kotlikoff, *Generational Accounting*, New York: Free Press, 1992.
A. Haeworth Robertson, *Social Security: What Every Taxpayer Should Know*, Washington: Retirement Policy Institute, 1992.

Chapter 8:
"Clinton Wants to Make Affluent Elderly Pay More for Social Security, Medicare," *Wall Street Journal*, June 10, 1992, p. A16.

"Democrats Are Outbidding One Another on Plans To Fight Recession by Rebuilding Infrastructure," *Wall Street Journal*, July 7, 1992, p. A14.

Theodore Forstmann, "Free Entrepreneurs to Fix the Economy," *Wall Street Journal*, March 31, 1992, p. A16.

"Middle Class Tax Squeeze," *Money*, April 1992, p. 80.

Gary and Aldona Robbins, *Capital, Taxes and Growth*, Dallas: National Center for Policy Analysis, 1992.

Chapter 9:
Aschauer, David A., "The Third Deficit," *The GAO Journal*, Spring 1991, p. 5.

Chapter 10:
Bill Archer, "Who's the Fairest of Them All?" *Policy Review*, Washington: Heritage Foundation, Summer 1991.

Charles Kadlec, "'Soak the Rich' Means the Middle Class Gets Wet," *Wall Street Journal*, Dec. 11, 1991, p. A16.

Michael Novak, "Getting the Message," *Forbes*, May 11, 1992, p.92.

Gary and Aldona Robbins, "Capital, Taxes and Growth," Dallas: National Center for Policy Analysis, January 1992.

Gary and Aldona Robbins, "Jerry Brown's Tax Plan," Dallas: National Center for Policy Analysis, April 1992.

"Taking Our Tax Temperature," *The American Enterprise*, Washington: American Enterprise Institute, Mar./Apr. 1992.

"Unpleasant Tax Surprises Sneak Up for a Bite," *Wall Street Journal*, Feb. 24, 1992, p. C1.

Tax Features, Washington: Tax Foundation, various issues, 1991 and 1992.

"Wealthier Taxpayers Will Take a Bigger Hit," *Wall Street Journal*, Nov. 20, 1991, p. C1.

Chapter 11:
Children's Well-Being: An International Comparison, U.S. Department of Commerce, Bureau of Census, International Population Reports, Series P-95, no. 80, 1990.

"How To Make Welfare Work," *Fortune*, June 1, 1992, p. 43.

"Income Dynamics," *Wall Street Journal*, June 16, 1992, p. A14.

"Low-Income Mobility Was High in 1980s," *Wall Street Journal*, June

2, 1992, p. A2.

Measuring the Effects of Benefits and Taxes on Income and Poverty: 1990, U.S. Department of Commerce, Bureau of Census, Current Population Reports, Consumer Income, Series P-60, no. 176-RD, 1991.

"Race Against Time," *The New Republic*, May 25, 1992, p. 7.

Trends in Income, by Selected Characteristics: 1964 to 1989, U.S. Department of Commerce, Bureau of Census, Current Population Reports, Consumer Income Series P-60, no. 177, 1991.

"What Should We Do About the Poor?" *Wall Street Journal*, April 14, 1992, p. A18.

Chapter 12:

Janet Currie and Nancy Cole, "Does Participation in Transfer Programs During Pregnancy Improve Birth Weight?" Working Paper No. 3832, National Bureau of Economic Research, Sept. 1991.

Nicholas Eberstadt, "America's Infant Mortality Problem: Parents," *Wall Street Journal*, Jan. 20, 1992, p. A12.

Thomas B. Edsall, "Race," *Atlantic Monthly*, May 1991, p. 53.

"The Kiplinger Washington Letter," Dec. 27, 1991.

Nicholas Lemann, "The Other Underclass," *Atlantic Monthly*, Dec. 1991, p. 96.

"Pain for the Poor, A Play for the Middle Class," *Business Week*, April 12, 1992, p. 31.

Robert Rector, "Food Fight: How Hungry Are America's Children?" *Policy Review*, Fall 1991, p. 38.

Debra J. Saunders, "Welfare Reform, California Style," *Wall Street Journal*, Feb. 25, 1992, p. A14.

Daniel J. Singal, "The Other Crisis in American Education," *Atlantic Monthly*, Nov. 1991, p. 59.

"State Spending," *Executive Alert*, Dallas: National Center for Policy Analysis, Mar./Apr. 1992, p. 3.

Claude M. Steele, "Race and the Schooling of Black Americans," *Atlantic Monthly*, April 1992, p. 68.

"What Should We Do About the Poor?" *Wall Street Journal*, April 14, 1992, p. A18.

Chapter 13:

"Perot Worries Corporate Titans But Appeals to Entrepreneurs," *Wall Street Journal*, June 18, 1992, p. B1.

Bruce Yandle, "Regulatory Reform in the Realm of the Rent Seekers," in Robert Mackey, et al., eds., *Public Choice: An Inside View of the*

FTC, Stanford: Hoover Press, 1987.

Chapter 14:
Robert Barro, "A Free Marketeer's Case Against Term Limits," *Wall Street Journal*, Dec. 24, 1991, p. A6.

"Business PACs," *Business Week*, June 22, 1992, p. 47.

"Can Term Limits Do the Job?" *U.S. News & World Report*, Nov. 11, 1991, p. 34.

John S. Fund, "Term Limitation," Policy Analysis 141, Washington: Cato Institute, October 30, 1990.

Paul A. Gigot, "Waxmangate: Why Americans Hate Congress," *Wall Street Journal*, June 19, 1992, p. A10.

Charles Kesler, "Limit Government, Not Terms," *Wall Street Journal*, August 1, 1991, p. A13.

Edward McFadden, "There's No Accounting for Congress," *The American Spectator*, July 1992, p. 24.

Arthur Schlesinger, "A Bad Idea, Whose Time Has Come," *Wall Street Journal*, Oct. 29, 1991, p. A22.

"Term Limits," *Business Week*, November 11, 1991, p. 40.

"Urban-Aid Legislation Exemplifies the Gridlock In Politics That Leaves U.S. Voters Frustrated," *Wall Street Journal*, July 1, 1992, p. A16.

Chapter 15:
Many organizations involved in term limits have helped make this book possible. They can be contacted for more information. The authors have no financial connection with any of these groups and do not endorse any of their particular activities.

National organizations directly involved in term limits include U.S. Term Limits at 800-733-6440 and 202-393-6440; the National Term Limits Campaign at 303-758-7343; and Term Limits Legal Institute at 202-371-0450.

ABOUT THE AUTHORS

Roger E. Meiners is Professor of Legal Studies and Director of the Center for Policy Studies at Clemson University. He is a graduate of Washington State University and the University of Arizona, and has a Ph.D. in economics from Virginia Tech and a law degree from the University of Miami. Dr. Meiners has been a member of the faculty at Texas A&M University, Emory University, and the University of Miami, and served as Director of the Atlanta office of the Federal Trade Commission. He is the author of numerous scholarly articles and books on political economy.

Roger LeRoy Miller is Research Director at the Center for Policy Studies at Clemson University. His undergraduate degree is from the University of California at Berkeley; his Ph.D. in economics is from the University of Chicago. He has taught at the University of Washington and the University of Miami, has been a consultant to numerous organizations, and been active in several businesses. Dr. Miller is one of the most prolific authors in the economics profession today, having authored numerous economics and public policy books.